2018 SQA Specimen and Past Papers with Answers

National 5
APPLICATIONS OF MATHEMATICS

2017 & 2018 Exams
and 2017 Specimen Question Paper

Hodder Gibson Study Skills Advice –
  National 5 Applications of Mathematics — page 3
Hodder Gibson Study Skills Advice – General — page 6
2017 EXAM (FOR LIFESKILLS MATHEMATICS) — page 9
2017 SPECIMEN QUESTION PAPER — page 45
2018 EXAM — page 85
ANSWERS — page 133

This book contains the official SQA 2017 Exam for National 5 Lifeskills Mathematics, and the 2017 Specimen Question Paper and official 2018 Exam for National 5 Applications of Mathematics, with associated SQA-approved answers modified from the official marking instructions that accompany the paper.

In addition the book contains study skills advice. This advice has been specially commissioned by Hodder Gibson, and has been written by experienced senior teachers and examiners in line with the new National 5 syllabus and assessment outlines. This is not SQA material but has been devised to provide further guidance for National 5 examinations.

Hodder Gibson is grateful to the copyright holders, as credited on the final page of the Answer section, for permission to use their material. Every effort has been made to trace the copyright holders and to obtain their permission for the use of copyright material. Hodder Gibson will be happy to receive information allowing us to rectify any error or omission in future editions.

Hachette UK's policy is to use papers that are natural, renewable and recyclable products and made from wood grown in sustainable forests. The logging and manufacturing processes are expected to conform to the environmental regulations of the country of origin.

Orders: please contact Bookpoint Ltd, 130 Park Drive, Milton Park, Abingdon, Oxon OX14 4SE. Telephone: (44) 01235 827827. Fax: (44) 01235 400454. Lines are open 9.00–5.00, Monday to Saturday, with a 24-hour message answering service. Visit our website at www.hoddereducation.co.uk. Hodder Gibson can also be contacted directly at hoddergibson@hodder.co.uk

This collection first published in 2018 by
Hodder Gibson, an imprint of Hodder Education,
An Hachette UK Company
211 St Vincent Street
Glasgow G2 5QY

National 5 2017 and 2018 Exam Papers and Answers; 2017 Specimen Question Paper and Answers © Scottish Qualifications Authority. Study Skills section © Hodder Gibson. All rights reserved. Apart from any use permitted under UK copyright law, no part of this publication may be reproduced or transmitted in any form or by any means, electronic or mechanical, including photocopying and recording, or held within any information storage and retrieval system, without permission in writing from the publisher or under licence from the Copyright Licensing Agency Limited. Further details of such licences (for reprographic reproduction) may be obtained from the Copyright Licensing Agency Limited, www.cla.co.uk

Typeset by Aptara, Inc.

Printed in the UK

A catalogue record for this title is available from the British Library

ISBN: 978-1-5104-5492-7

2 1

2019 2018

Introduction

National 5 Applications of Mathematics (formerly Lifeskills Mathematics)

This book of SQA Past Papers contains the question papers used in the 2017 Lifeskills Mathematics and 2018 Applications of Mathematics exams (with answers at the back of the book). A specimen question paper reflecting the content and duration of the exam in 2018 is also included.

All of the question papers included in the book provide excellent representative exam practice for the final exams. Using these papers as part of your revision will help you to develop the vital skills and techniques needed for the exam, and will help you to identify any knowledge gaps you may have.

It is always a very good idea to refer to SQA's website for the most up-to-date course specification documents. These are available at https://www.sqa.org.uk/sqa/81281

The course

The Applications of Mathematics (formerly Lifeskills Mathematics) course is a qualification which focuses on the application of mathematical skills in real-life contexts.

The National 5 Applications of Mathematics course aims to enable you to develop:

- a range of mathematical techniques and apply these to real-life problems or situations
- the ability to analyse a range of real-life problems or situations
- a confident and independent approach towards the use of mathematics in real-life situations
- the ability to select, apply and combine mathematical skills to new or unfamiliar situations in life and work
- the ability to use mathematical reasoning skills to generalise, support arguments, draw conclusions, assess risk and make informed decisions
- the ability to analyse, interpret and present a range of information
- the ability to communicate mathematical information in a variety of forms
- the ability to think creatively and in abstract ways.

Before starting this course you should already have the knowledge, understanding and skills required to achieve a pass in National 4 Applications of Mathematics and/or be proficient in appropriate experiences and outcomes.

This course enables you to further develop your knowledge, understanding, skills and reasoning processes in personal finance, statistics, geometry, measure, numeracy and data. The table outlines the topics covered in each area of the course:

Financial Skills	Statistical Skills	Numeracy Skills
Budgeting	Investigate probability/risk	Select and use appropriate notation and units
Income and pay slips	Statistical diagrams	
Tax and deductions	Analyse/compare data sets	Select and carry out operations including:
Best deal	Line of best fit	
Currency conversion		• working to given decimal places
Interest rates and saving/borrowing		• rounding to given significant figures
Geometrical Skills	**Graphical Data and Probability Skills**	• fractions and mixed numbers
Gradient	Extract/interpret data from at least three different graphical forms	• percentages, including compound
Composite shapes: Area		• speed, distance, time
Composite solids: Volume		• area
Pythagoras' theorem	Make/justify decisions based on interpretation of data	• volume
Measurement Skills		• ratio
Scale drawing	Make/justify decisions based on probability	• proportion, direct and indirect
Bearings		
Container packing		
Precedence tables		
Time management		
Tolerance		

You will use your reasoning skills and the skills above, linked to real-life contexts. The amount of reasoning is what makes Applications of Mathematics different. You will be asked to analyse, compare, justify and communicate information.

Assessment

Course assessment for Applications of Mathematics is based on a final exam paper. The number of marks and the times allotted for the examination papers are as follows:

Paper 1 (non-calculator)   45 marks   1 hour and 5 minutes

Paper 2 (calculator allowed)   65 marks   2 hours

The Award is graded A–D, with the grade being determined by your performance in the exam, i.e. based on the total mark out of 110.

To achieve a grade C; you will typically have demonstrated **successful** performance in relation to the skills, knowledge and understanding of the course.

To achieve a grade A; you will typically have demonstrated a **consistently high level** of performance in relation to the skills, knowledge and understanding of the course.

Paper 1 consists of short-answer and extended-response questions, most of which are in context.

Paper 2 consists of short-answer questions, extended-response questions and **case studies**, most of which are in context. The time given to this Paper allows you to read and absorb the information in the case studies.

Some tips for achieving a good mark

- **DOING** maths questions is the most effective use of your study time. You will benefit much more from spending 30 minutes doing maths questions than spending several hours copying out notes or reading a maths textbook.

- Practise doing the types of questions that are likely to appear in the exam. Use the marking instructions to check your answers and to understand what the examiners are looking for. Ask your teacher for help if you get stuck.

- **SHOW ALL WORKING CLEARLY.** The instructions on the front of the exam paper state that "To earn full marks you must show your working in your answers". A "correct" answer with no working may only be awarded partial marks or even no marks at all. An incomplete answer will be awarded marks for any appropriate working. Attempt every question, even if you are not sure whether you are correct or not. Your solution may contain working which will gain some marks. A blank response is certain to be awarded no marks. Never score out working unless you have something better to replace it with.

- Reasoning skills are a major part of Applications of Mathematics. One way of showing your reasoning process is by showing all of your working. Quite often you will be asked to *"Use your working to justify your answer"* – so you cannot just say "yes" or "no" without your working.

- Communication is very important in presenting solutions to questions. Diagrams are often a good way of conveying information and enabling markers to understand your working. Where a diagram is included in a question, it is often good practice to mark in any dimensions etc, which you work out and may use later.

- In Paper 1, you have to carry out calculations without a calculator. Ensure that you practise your number skills regularly, especially within questions that test course content. Also make sure that after you have calculated an answer you state the **units**, if appropriate. Paper 1 will be a mixture of short, medium and extended questions covering a single "skill", to three or four skills selected from the table on page 4. Most questions will be in context.

- In Paper 2, you will be allowed to use a calculator. Always use **your own** calculator. Different calculators often function in slightly different ways, so make sure that you know how to operate yours. Having to use a calculator that you are unfamiliar with on the day of the exam may cause frustration and loss of time. Paper 2 consists of short-answer questions, extended-response questions and case studies, most of which will be in context.

- Prepare thoroughly to tackle questions from **all** parts of the course. Always try all parts of a question: Just because you could not complete part (a), for example, does not mean you could not do part (b) or (c).

- Look at how many **marks** are allocated to a question – this will give you an idea of how much work is required. The more marks, the more work!

- Look for **key words** in questions: state, calculate, compare, plot, sketch, draw, justify.

Some areas to consider

Each question is likely to have a mixture of strategy, process and communication marks.

You will be expected to:

- select a strategy (there may be more than one way to do a question)

Here are some examples to consider:

- process the information (for example, carry out a calculation)
- communicate your answer (for example, "yes the company would accept as tolerance is within limits").

Types of question	Things to consider
You may be asked to mark points on a scatter diagram, draw a line of best fit and then compare it with one already drawn.	Ensure points are **plotted accurately**. Try to make the **"slope"** of the line match points. Try to have about the same number of points above and below the line of best fit.
You may be asked to make a scale drawing of, for example, a garden. You may then be asked to calculate measurements from this drawing.	Choose a scale which gives a good size, to fit the space given to you. **State the scale** you have used. Use this scale to calculate actual sizes. Remember to **state units**.
You may be asked to construct a box plot. You may have to compare this with one given.	Make sure you have a scale clearly marked. Make sure you mark in the **five-figure summary**. Valid comparison: 1 mark equals one comparison, 2 marks equal two comparison statements. For example, "plot 2 has a higher median and a greater spread". L Q1 Q2 Q3 H 10 15 20 25 30 35 40 45 50

In Paper 2 you have been given more time to allow you to read and absorb the information, particularly in the case studies.

You should take the opportunity to "settle into" the Paper by carefully working through the short-answer and extended-response questions. This will get you "thinking mathematically".

You should then look through the case studies to get a "feel" for what they are asking.

Case studies will typically "flow" through a context or scenario; developing the theme and assessing a variety of skills, knowledge and understanding. The case studies will vary in length; some assessing one, or one or two skills, whilst longer ones will test a number of skills across the range of skills in the course.

Typically you will be given a context and have to answer a question or two on the information given. You may then be given more information in order that the case study may develop and you will have another part of the question to answer. In this way you should be able to build up your answers and, therefore, your marks as you progress through the case study.

Remember, even if you could not answer, say, part (b) – always look at part (c) to see if you can answer that part.

Good luck!

Remember that the rewards for passing National 5 Applications of Mathematics are well worth it! Your pass will help you get the future you want for yourself. In the exam, be confident in your own ability. If you're not sure how to answer a question, trust your instincts and just give it a go anyway. Keep calm and don't panic! GOOD LUCK!

Study Skills – what you need to know to pass exams!

General exam revision: 20 top tips

When preparing for exams, it is easy to feel unsure of where to start or how to revise. This guide to general exam revision provides a good starting place, and, as these are very general tips, they can be applied to all your exams.

1. Start revising in good time.

Don't leave revision until the last minute – this will make you panic and it will be difficult to learn. Make a revision timetable that counts down the weeks to go.

2. Work to a study plan.

Set up sessions of work spread through the weeks ahead. Make sure each session has a focus and a clear purpose. What will you study, when and why? Be realistic about what you can achieve in each session, and don't be afraid to adjust your plans as needed.

3. Make sure you know exactly when your exams are.

Get your exam dates from the SQA website and use the timetable builder tool to create your own exam schedule. You will also get a personalised timetable from your school, but this might not be until close to the exam period.

4. Make sure that you know the topics that make up each course.

Studying is easier if material is in manageable chunks – why not use the SQA topic headings or create your own from your class notes? Ask your teacher for help on this if you are not sure.

5. Break the chunks up into even smaller bits.

The small chunks should be easier to cope with. Remember that they fit together to make larger ideas. Even the process of chunking down will help!

6. Ask yourself these key questions for each course:

- Are all topics compulsory or are there choices?
- Which topics seem to come up time and time again?
- Which topics are your strongest and which are your weakest?

Use your answers to these questions to work out how much time you will need to spend revising each topic.

7. Make sure you know what to expect in the exam.

The subject-specific introduction to this book will help with this. Make sure you can answer these questions:

- How is the paper structured?
- How much time is there for each part of the exam?
- What types of question are involved? These will vary depending on the subject so read the subject-specific section carefully.

8. Past papers are a vital revision tool!

Use past papers to support your revision wherever possible. This book contains the answers and mark schemes too – refer to these carefully when checking your work. Using the mark scheme is useful; even if you don't manage to get all the marks available first time when you first practise, it helps you identify how to extend and develop your answers to get more marks next time – and of course, in the real exam.

9. Use study methods that work well for you.

People study and learn in different ways. Reading and looking at diagrams suits some students. Others prefer to listen and hear material – what about reading out loud or getting a friend or family member to do this for you? You could also record and play back material.

10. There are three tried and tested ways to make material stick in your long-term memory:

- Practising – e.g. rehearsal, repeating
- Organising – e.g. making drawings, lists, diagrams, tables, memory aids
- Elaborating – e.g. incorporating the material into a story or an imagined journey

11. Learn actively.

Most people prefer to learn actively – for example, making notes, highlighting, redrawing and redrafting, making up memory aids, or writing past paper answers. A good way to stay engaged and inspired is to mix and match these methods – find the combination that best suits you. This is likely to vary depending on the topic or subject.

12. Be an expert.

Be sure to have a few areas in which you feel you are an expert. This often works because at least some of them will come up, which can boost confidence.

13. Try some visual methods.

Use symbols, diagrams, charts, flashcards, post-it notes etc. Don't forget – the brain takes in chunked images more easily than loads of text.

14. Remember – practice makes perfect.

Work on difficult areas again and again. Look and read – then test yourself. You cannot do this too much.

15. Try past papers against the clock.

Practise writing answers in a set time. This is a good habit from the start but is especially important when you get closer to exam time.

16. Collaborate with friends.

Test each other and talk about the material – this can really help. Two brains are better than one! It is amazing how talking about a problem can help you solve it.

17. Know your weaknesses.

Ask your teacher for help to identify what you don't know. Try to do this as early as possible. If you are having trouble, it is probably with a difficult topic, so your teacher will already be aware of this – most students will find it tough.

18. Have your materials organised and ready.

Know what is needed for each exam:
- Do you need a calculator or a ruler?
- Should you have pencils as well as pens?
- Will you need water or paper tissues?

19. Make full use of school resources.

Find out what support is on offer:
- Are there study classes available?
- When is the library open?
- When is the best time to ask for extra help?
- Can you borrow textbooks, study guides, past papers, etc.?
- Is school open for Easter revision?

20. Keep fit and healthy!

Try to stick to a routine as much as possible, including with sleep. If you are tired, sluggish or dehydrated, it is difficult to see how concentration is even possible. Combine study with relaxation, drink plenty of water, eat sensibly, and get fresh air and exercise – all these things will help more than you could imagine. Good luck!

NATIONAL 5
2017

N5
National Qualifications 2017

FOR OFFICIAL USE

Mark

X744/75/01

**Lifeskills Mathematics
Paper 1 (Non-Calculator)**

MONDAY, 29 MAY
1:00 PM – 1:50 PM

Fill in these boxes and read what is printed below.

Full name of centre

Town

Forename(s)

Surname

Number of seat

Date of birth
Day Month Year

Scottish candidate number

Total marks — 35

Attempt ALL questions.

You may NOT use a calculator.

Full credit will be given only to solutions which contain appropriate working.

State the units for your answer where appropriate.

Write your answers clearly in the spaces provided in this booklet. Additional space for answers is provided at the end of this booklet. If you use this space you must clearly identify the question number you are attempting.

Use **blue** or **black** ink.

Before leaving the examination room you must give this book to the Invigilator; if you do not, you may lose all the marks for this paper.

FORMULAE LIST

Circumference of a circle: $C = \pi d$

Area of a circle: $A = \pi r^2$

Theorem of Pythagoras:

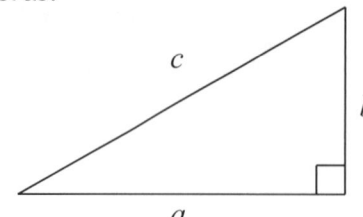

$a^2 + b^2 = c^2$

Volume of a cylinder: $V = \pi r^2 h$

Volume of a prism: $V = Ah$

Volume of a cone: $V = \frac{1}{3}\pi r^2 h$

Volume of a sphere: $V = \frac{4}{3}\pi r^3$

Standard deviation: $s = \sqrt{\dfrac{\Sigma(x-\bar{x})^2}{n-1}} = \sqrt{\dfrac{\Sigma x^2 - (\Sigma x)^2/n}{n-1}}$, where n is the sample size.

Gradient:

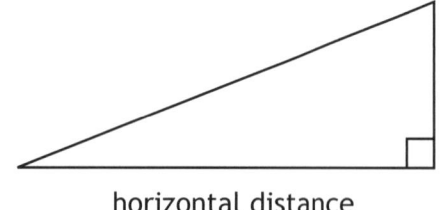

$$\text{gradient} = \frac{\text{vertical height}}{\text{horizontal distance}}$$

Total marks — 35

Attempt ALL questions

1. A wall is built using foam bricks which are 194 ± 2 mm long.

   The wall is 50 bricks long.

   What is the minimum length of the wall? **2**

2. Anna works as a sales person for a computer company.

   She is paid a basic monthly salary of £2450 plus commission of 2·5% on her monthly sales over £3000.

   (a) Calculate Anna's gross salary for April when her sales totalled £9000. **3**

   In her April payslip, she has the following deductions:

   - Income Tax   £334·67
   - National Insurance   £230·20
   - Pension   £164·74

   (b) Calculate her net salary for April. **2**

Page three [Turn over

3. Scott is a farmer.

   He records the weight of a calf from birth.

   The weight of his calf is shown in the table below.

Days after birth	0	60	120	160	200	260
Weight (kg)	40	110	130	175	220	275

   (a) On the grid below draw a scatter graph to show this data.

   (An additional grid, if required, can be found on *Page fourteen*.)

   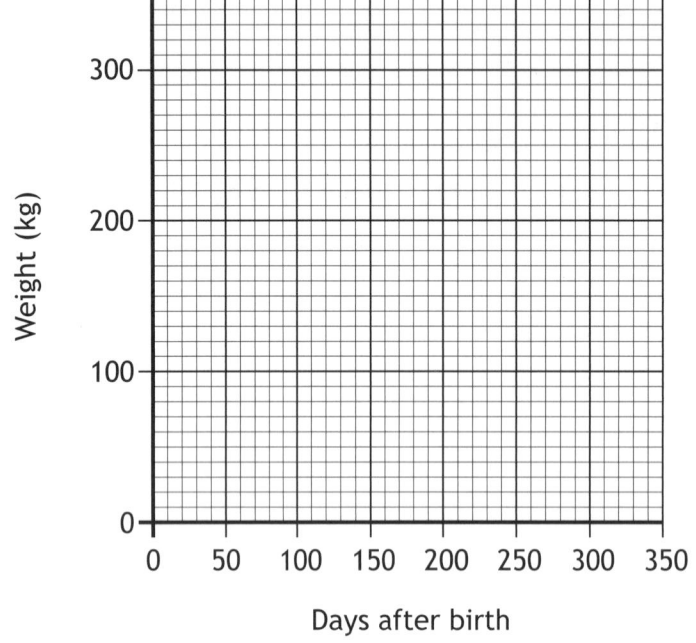

   (b) Draw a line of best fit on the diagram above.

   (c) Use your line of best fit to estimate the **age** of this calf in days when it weighed 240 kilograms.

4. When classifying mountain bike trails, the gradient of the steepest section is taken into account.

Colour Grade (Difficulty)	Maximum Gradient
Green (Easy)	$\frac{1}{10}$
Blue (Intermediate)	$\frac{3}{20}$
Red (Advanced)	$\frac{1}{4}$
Black (Severe)	$\frac{1}{2}$

A new trail has been built at a mountain bike centre.

The steepest section of the new trail is shown below.

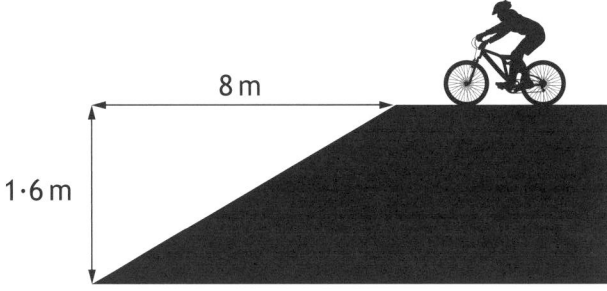

Can this be classified as a blue trail?

Use your working to justify your answer.

3

5. Jane is trying to improve the number of pull ups she can do.

   She looks online for pull up assistance bands.

   Jane finds a table explaining which type of bands she should use based on her weight and the number of unassisted pull ups she can do.

   The table is shown below.

	Body Weight (pounds)					
Unassisted pull ups	90–120	121–150	151–200	201–250	251–300	300+
0–4	D	D and A	E	F	F	G and A
5–8	C and A	D	E	E	E and B	G
9–11	C	D	D and C	E	E and A	F
12–15	C	C and B	D and B	D and C	E	E and C
16–20	B	C	D	D and B	E	E

   Jane weighs herself. She is 10 stone and 1 pound.

   1 stone = 14 pounds

   Jane can do 3 unassisted pull ups.

   (a) Which band(s) does the table recommend that Jane should buy?   1

5. (continued)

Jane's personal trainer, Lynn, wants to buy one of each band A to G.

The recommended retail prices (RRP) of the bands are shown in the table below.

Band	Colour	RRP
A	Yellow	£2·50
B	Red	£3·90
C	Black	£8·95
D	Purple	£10·95
E	Green	£14·00
F	Blue	£17·00
G	Orange	£18·50

To buy all of the bands individually, the total RRP would be £75·80.

Lynn considers the following special offers.

Shop 1

Buy orange, blue, and green bands at RRP

Shop 2

Shop 3

(b) Which shop offers the cheapest option for buying one of each band? 3

Use your working to justify your answer.

6. The mathematics teachers in a school win a lottery.

They decide to share their winnings **in proportion to** the amount they each pay per week.

They each pay the following amounts per week:

Mr Jones	£0·50
Miss Smith	£2·00
Mr Ross	£2·50
Mr Young	£4·00

Mr Young's share is £2 794 000.

Calculate how much the teachers win in total.

7. Aneesa makes enamelled badges.

   Each badge is made from metal.

   The shape of the badge is shown below.

   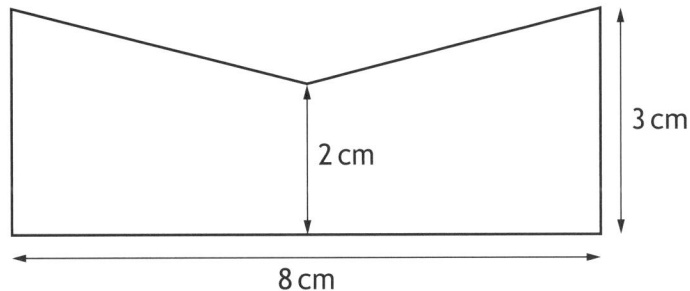

   (a) Calculate the area of the front of each badge. 2

   The front of each badge is covered with enamel.

   The enamel that Aneesa buys costs £90 for one pack.

   One pack will cover 180 cm².

   She makes as many badges as possible from one pack.

   The metal that she uses costs £3 for each badge.

   To make a profit, Aneesa adds an extra £17 to the cost of each badge.

   (b) Calculate her selling price for each badge. 3

8. Natalie is donating blood.

   Whilst donating blood she notices a chart.

   The chart states that not every blood type can be given to every patient.

   The table shows which patients each blood type can help.

   Blood type can be either positive (+) or negative (−).

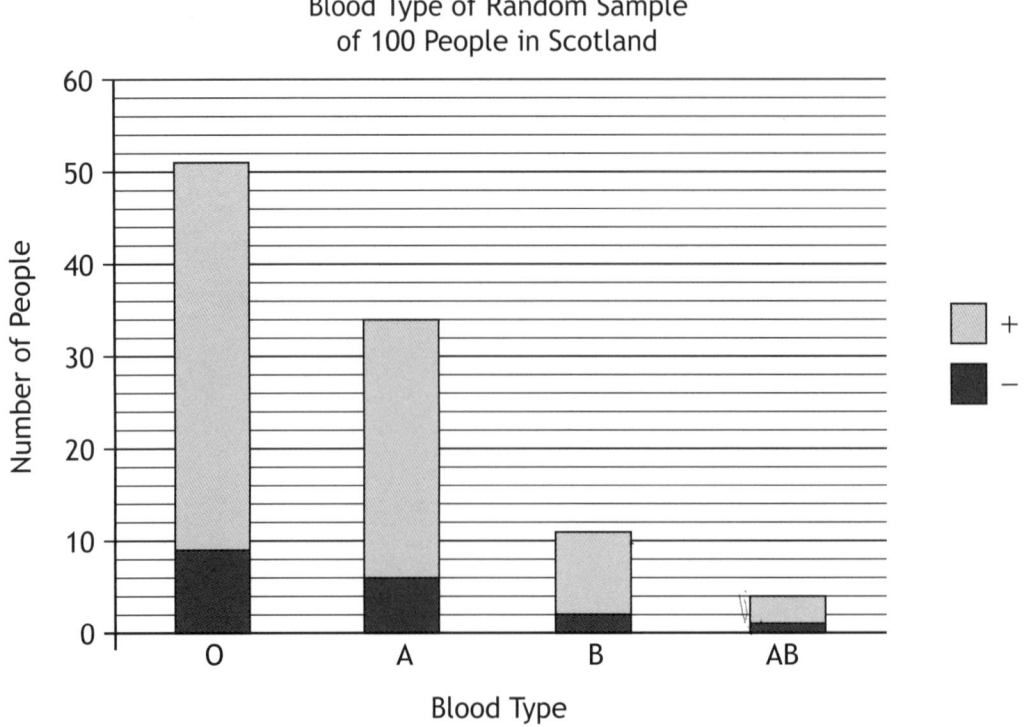

   For example the blood of a donor with blood type AB− can only be given safely to a patient with blood type AB+ or AB−.

   Natalie then notices a graph showing the blood type of a random sample of **100** people in Scotland.

8. (continued)

Natalie's blood type is B+.

What fraction of the people sampled could safely be given Natalie's blood?   3

9. A new design is discussed for a glue dispenser.

   It is to be made from two plates of plastic.

   Each plate is in the shape of a right angled triangle and a semi-circle as shown.

   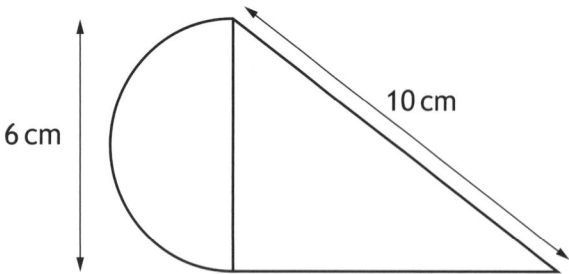

   (a) Calculate the perimeter of each plate.

   Use π = 3·14.

9. (continued)

A rectangular piece of plastic 0·5 cm wide is bent and wrapped around the perimeter of the two plates to join them together.

The rectangular piece of plastic will be 0·3 cm shorter than the perimeter of the shape to allow the glue to flow.

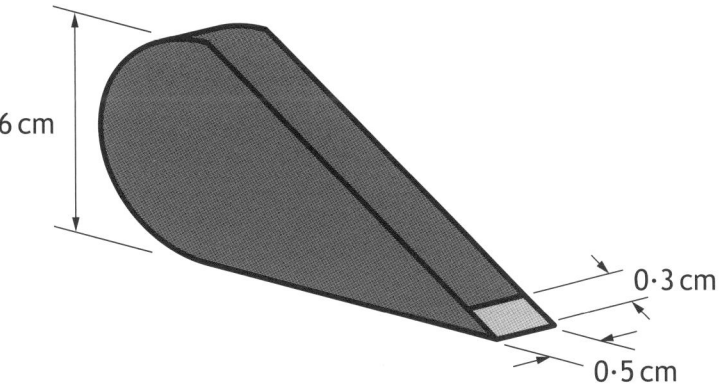

(b) Calculate the area of the **rectangular** piece of plastic required to hold the plates together.

2

[END OF QUESTION PAPER]

ADDITIONAL SPACE FOR ANSWERS

Additional grid for Question 3 (a)

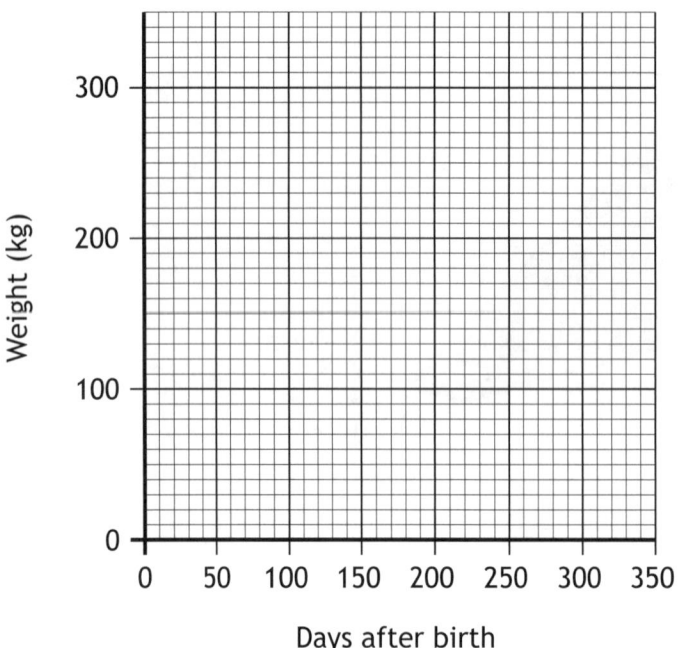

ADDITIONAL SPACE FOR ANSWERS

ADDITIONAL SPACE FOR ANSWERS

FOR OFFICIAL USE

N5 National Qualifications 2017

Mark

X744/75/02

Lifeskills Mathematics
Paper 2

MONDAY, 29 MAY
2:10 PM — 3:50 PM

Fill in these boxes and read what is printed below.

Full name of centre

Town

Forename(s)

Surname

Number of seat

Date of birth

Day Month Year

Scottish candidate number

Total marks — 55

Attempt ALL questions.

You may use a calculator.

Full credit will be given only to solutions which contain appropriate working.

State the units for your answer where appropriate.

Write your answers clearly in the spaces provided in this booklet. Additional space for answers is provided at the end of this booklet. If you use this space you must clearly identify the question number you are attempting.

Use **blue** or **black** ink.

Before leaving the examination room you must give this book to the Invigilator; if you do not, you may lose all the marks for this paper.

FORMULAE LIST

Circumference of a circle: $C = \pi d$

Area of a circle: $A = \pi r^2$

Theorem of Pythagoras:

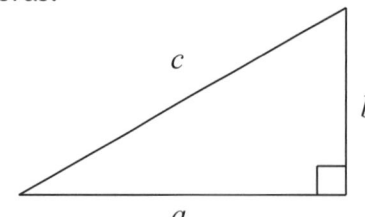

$a^2 + b^2 = c^2$

Volume of a cylinder: $V = \pi r^2 h$

Volume of a prism: $V = Ah$

Volume of a cone: $V = \frac{1}{3}\pi r^2 h$

Volume of a sphere: $V = \frac{4}{3}\pi r^3$

Standard deviation: $s = \sqrt{\dfrac{\Sigma(x-\bar{x})^2}{n-1}} = \sqrt{\dfrac{\Sigma x^2 - (\Sigma x)^2/n}{n-1}}$, where n is the sample size.

Gradient:

$$\text{gradient} = \frac{\text{vertical height}}{\text{horizontal distance}}$$

Total marks — 55

Attempt ALL questions

1. The Victorians used stoneware hot water bottles.

   They were semi-circular prisms as shown.

   The diameter of the bottle is 14 cm and the length is 30 cm.

   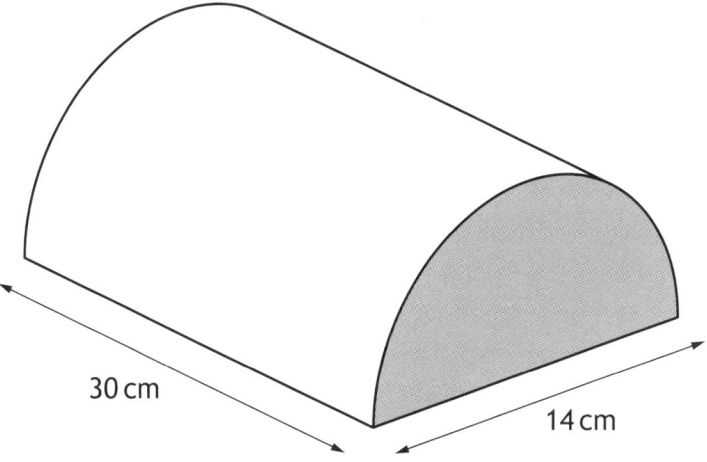

   Calculate the volume of the hot water bottle. 3

2. Asif bought 8000 shares in a local company in April 2013.

   Each share cost him 73 pence.

   The value of the shares
   - decreased by 3% in the first year then,
   - increased by 4·2% in each of the next **two years**.

   (a) How much were Asif's shares worth in total in April 2016? **5**

   In April 2017 Asif's shares were worth £6560 in total.

   He decided to sell 5000 of his shares.

   He was charged £12·95 commission on his sale.

   (b) How much did he receive from the sale of the shares? **2**

3. Kyle is buying a new three piece suite.

It is advertised at a price of £1260.

3 PIECE SUITE FOR SALE

£1260

Kyle can't afford to pay this all at once.

He decides to use a payment plan to buy the three piece suite.

The **total price** of the payment plan is **12% more** than the advertised price.

The payments are calculated as follows:

- deposit of $\frac{1}{3}$ of the total price
- 8 equal monthly instalments
- final payment of £200.

How much will each monthly instalment be?

4. The back to back stem and leaf diagram shows data gathered at a gymnasium before and after walking on a treadmill.

Heart rate data (beats per minute (bpm))

Before   After

```
    9 8 3 2 0 | 5 | 9
6 6 6 1 1 0 0 | 6 | 2 4 7 8 8          7|8 = 78
        9 6 2 | 7 | 1 1 1 8
              | 8 | 2 4 9
              | 9 | 2 5
```

n = 15   n = 15

(a) State the most common heart rate (bpm) **after** walking on the treadmill. 1

(b) What is the difference in the median heart rates (bpm) before and after walking on the treadmill? 2

4. (continued)

(c) Construct a boxplot to show the heart rate data **after** exercise. 4

(An additional diagram, if required, can be found on *Page sixteen*.)

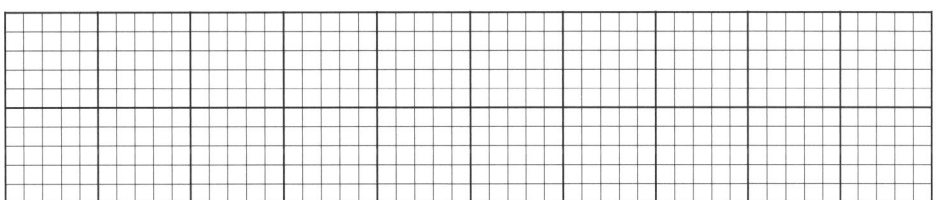

5. Mr and Mrs Sibbald went on a cruise.

   Part of the cruise involved sailing from Villefranche to Livorno.

   The map below shows the route the ship takes.

   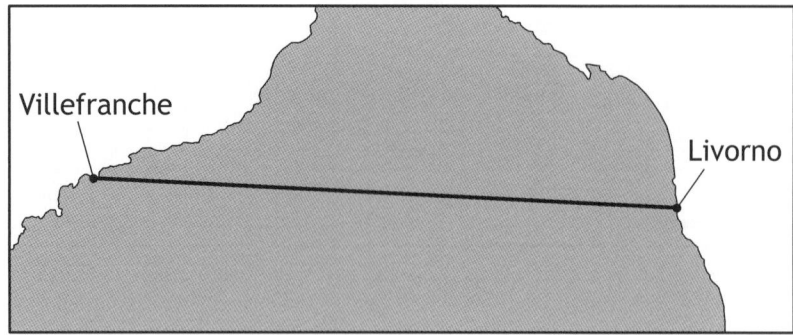

   The scale of the map is 1 : 3 000 000

   (a) Calculate the distance from Villefranche to Livorno.

   Give your answer in kilometres.

   It took 7 hours and 30 minutes to sail from Villefranche to Livorno.

   (b) Calculate the average speed of the ship's journey.

   Give your answer in knots.

   1 kilometre per hour = 0·54 knots

   Round your answer to 2 significant figures.

5. (continued)

Mr and Mrs Sibbald took £2400 spending money.

They exchanged 55% of their money into euro, to spend ashore.

The exchange rate was £1 = 1·15 euro.

By the end of the cruise they had spent 1379 euro.

(c) Calculate how many euro they had left at the end of the cruise. 2

Mr and Mrs Sibbald take part in an on board lottery which consists of a draw from a set of 32 balls numbered from 1 to 32.

(d) (i) What is the probability that the first ball drawn has a number greater than 25? 1

In the draw four numbered balls are drawn and not replaced.

A further bonus ball is also drawn.

(ii) What is the probability of the number 9 being drawn as the bonus ball if it was not drawn in the first four? 2

6. Russell is a lorry driver for a mail delivery company.

The mail is packed into cages which are then loaded on to the lorry.

His lorry has two levels for fitting cages.

Each cage has wheels on the bottom and must always be **loaded upright**.

The dimensions of the cage and the internal dimensions of the back of the lorry are shown in the diagrams.

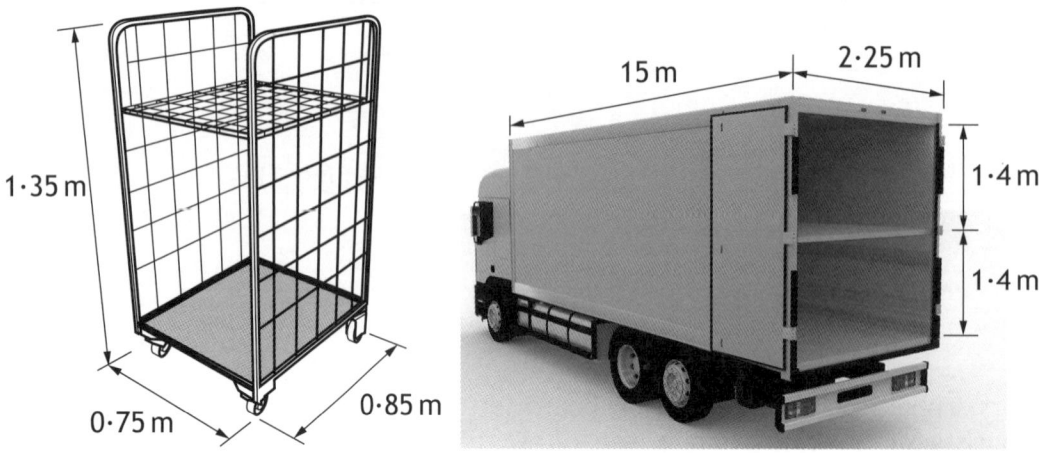

(a) What is the maximum number of cages that can be loaded into the back of the lorry? **3**

6. **(continued)**

   Russell works night shift.
   - He works from 2300 until 0900 the next day.
   - His rate of pay is £14·40 per hour.
   - He gets paid time and a half between 2200 and 0730.
   - He works 5 shifts each week.

   (b) Calculate his weekly gross pay. 3

7. Mr Mackenzie has decided to move to South Africa with his family. He has been offered jobs in both Durban and Cape Town.

The typical monthly temperatures from March to August in Durban are recorded in the table below.

Month	Temperature (°C)
March	24
April	22
May	19
June	18
July	17
August	17

(a) For the typical monthly temperatures in Durban, calculate:

(i) the mean; **1**

(ii) the standard deviation. **3**

7. (continued)

In Cape Town the mean monthly temperature for the same period is 15·5 °C and the standard deviation is 1·87 °C.

(b) Make two valid comments comparing the temperatures in both cities. **2**

Mr Mackenzie accepts the job in Durban.

As part of his job he is in contact with the London, New York and Mumbai offices of the company he works for.

He is planning a conference call at 3:30 pm the following day, from his office in Durban.

At 17:25 he noticed the clocks on the wall of his office showed the times below.

| 10:25 | 15:25 | 17:25 | 22:55 |
| New York | London | Durban | Mumbai |

All offices work 08:00 to 18:00 local time.

(c) Which offices are available to take part in the conference call? **3**

8. Zuzanna is remodelling her shower room.

She considers two designs.

The first design has a pentagonal shower tray.

The door will be fitted on the side of the tray as shown.

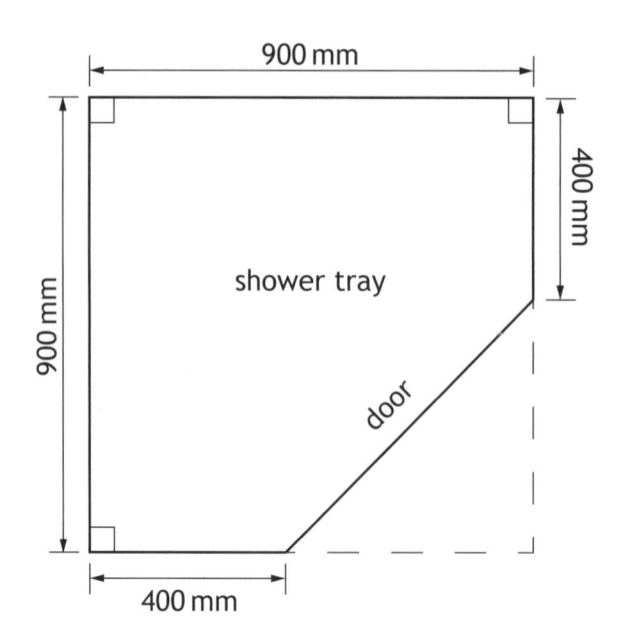

(a) Calculate the length of the side where the door will go. **3**

(b) Calculate the area of the pentagonal shower tray. **2**

8. (continued)

The second design that Zuzanna is considering is the offset quadrant shower tray shown below.

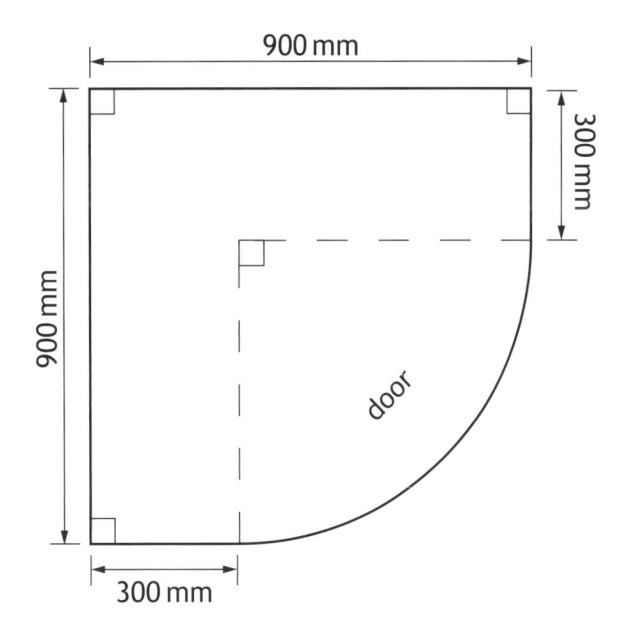

The offset quadrant design has quarter of a circle forming part of the edge.

(c) Zuzanna will choose the design that gives the greater area.

Which design will Zuzanna choose, the pentagonal or the offset quadrant shower tray? 4

Use your working to justify your answer.

[END OF QUESTION PAPER]

ADDITIONAL SPACE FOR ANSWERS

Additional diagram for use in Question 4 (c).

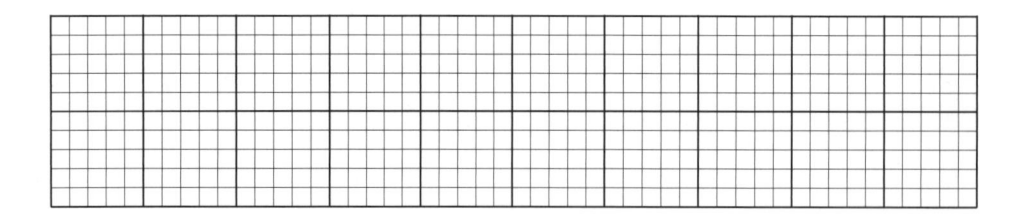

ADDITIONAL SPACE FOR ANSWERS

ADDITIONAL SPACE FOR ANSWERS

NATIONAL 5

2017 Specimen Question Paper

N5

National Qualifications
SPECIMEN ONLY

FOR OFFICIAL USE

Mark

S844/75/01

**Applications of Mathematics
Paper 1 (Non-Calculator)**

Date — Not applicable

Duration — 1 hour 5 minutes

Fill in these boxes and read what is printed below.

Full name of centre

Town

Forename(s)

Surname

Number of seat

Date of birth
Day Month Year

Scottish candidate number

Total marks — 45

Attempt ALL questions.

You may NOT use a calculator.

To earn full marks you must show your working in your answers.

State the units for your answer where appropriate.

Write your answers clearly in the spaces provided in this booklet. Additional space for answers is provided at the end of this booklet. If you use this space you must clearly identify the question number you are attempting.

Use **blue** or **black** ink.

Before leaving the examination room you must give this booklet to the Invigilator; if you do not, you may lose all the marks for this paper.

SQA

FORMULAE LIST

Circumference of a circle: $C = \pi d$

Area of a circle: $A = \pi r^2$

Theorem of Pythagoras:

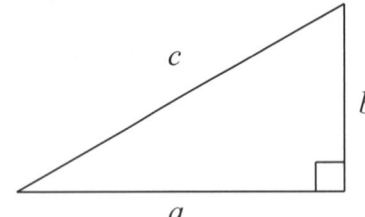

$$a^2 + b^2 = c^2$$

Volume of a cylinder: $V = \pi r^2 h$

Volume of a prism: $V = Ah$

Volume of a cone: $V = \frac{1}{3}\pi r^2 h$

Volume of a sphere: $V = \frac{4}{3}\pi r^3$

Standard deviation: $s = \sqrt{\dfrac{\Sigma(x-\bar{x})^2}{n-1}} = \sqrt{\dfrac{\Sigma x^2 - (\Sigma x)^2/n}{n-1}}$, where n is the sample size.

Gradient:

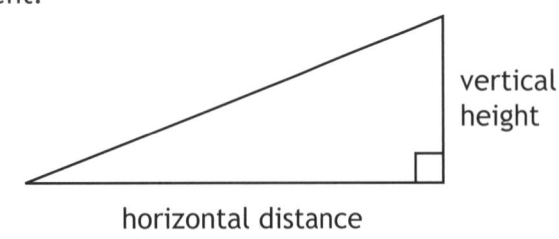

$$\text{gradient} = \frac{\text{vertical height}}{\text{horizontal distance}}$$

Total marks — 45

Attempt ALL questions

1. Liam is on holiday in New York.

   He looks at the world time app on his phone.

   The display shows the times below:

   New York 5:30pm

   Glasgow 10:30pm

   His flight to Glasgow departs New York at 8:00 am local time.

   The flight time is 6 hours 30 minutes.

   Calculate the local time when the plane lands in Glasgow. **2**

2. S6 pupils were asked to choose their favourite subject.

The results are shown in the table below.

Subject	Boys	Girls
Geography	11	7
French	9	14
Maths	18	13
Spanish	10	12
Modern Studies	18	8
Total	66	54

Calculate the probability that a boy from this group chose French as his favourite subject.

Give your answer as a fraction in its simplest form. 2

3. A company orders a bag of washers with a thickness of $2 \cdot 4 \pm 0 \cdot 05$ mm.

An inspector takes a sample from the bag of washers.

The thicknesses, in mm, of the washers in this sample are shown below.

2·44, 2·37, 2·36, 2·45, 2·35

2·35, 2·44, 2·43, 2·34, 2·40

2·40, 2·41, 2·39, 2·38, 2·46

2·41, 2·39, 2·53, 2·36, 2·37

For the bag to be accepted, at least 88% of the washers in this sample must be within tolerance.

Will the bag be accepted? 3

4. The table below shows the vehicle tax to be paid on different vehicles.

The amount of vehicle tax paid depends on the CO_2 emissions of the vehicle and the fuel type.

| | | Tax for Petrol and Diesel Cars ||||
| | | Non Direct Debit || Direct Debit |||
Bands	CO_2 emission figure (g/km)	12 months	Six months	Single 12 month payment	Total payable by 12 monthly instalments	Single six month payment
Band A	Up to 100	£0	–	–	–	–
Band B	101 to 110	£20	–	£20	£21	–
Band C	111 to 120	£30	–	£30	£31·50	–
Band D	121 to 130	£110	£60·50	£110	£115·50	£57·75
Band E	131 to 140	£130	£71·50	£130	£136·50	£68·25
Band F	141 to 150	£145	£79·75	£145	£152·25	£76·13
Band G	151 to 165	£180	£99	£180	£189	£94·50
Band H	166 to 175	£205	£112·75	£205	£215·25	£107·63
Band I	176 to 185	£225	£123·75	£225	£236·25	£118·13
Band J	186 to 200	£265	£145·75	£265	£278·25	£139·13
Band K	201 to 225	£290	£159·50	£290	£304·50	£152·25
Band L	226 to 255	£490	£269·50	£490	£514·50	£257·25
Band M	Over 255	£505	£277·75	£505	£530·25	£265·13

Tom buys a petrol car which has a CO_2 emission figure of 142 g/km.

Tom decides to pay his vehicle tax by direct debit in two single six month payments.

How much more expensive is this than a single 12 month payment by direct debit?

3

5. This back-to-back stem and leaf diagram represents the number of hours a class spends on social networking websites in a week.

```
          Girls |   | Boys
                | 0 | 3 6 8 9
         8 4 3 0| 1 | 1 2 4 7 7 8 9
     9 8 7 6 2 2 1| 2 | 2 6 7 8 8
             7 2 0| 3 |
                 2| 4 |

          n = 15        n = 16
```

KEY

3 | 1   represents 13 hours
  | 2 | 5   represents 25 hours

(a) A boxplot is drawn to represent one set of data.

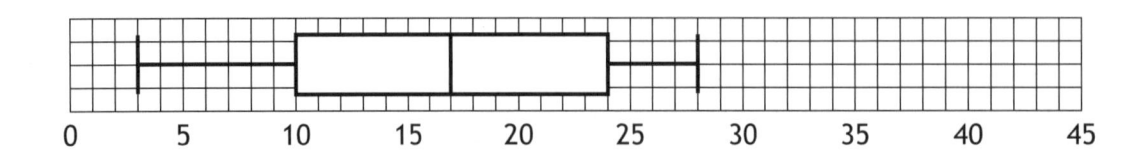

Which set of data does this represent?

Give a reason for your answer.   **1**

(b) For the other set of data, state:

the median

the lower quartile

the upper quartile.   **2**

5. (continued)

(c) Construct a box plot for the second set of data.

(An additional diagram, if required, can be found on *Page sixteen*.)

0   5   10   15   20   25   30   35   40   45

6. Mo is an electrician.

The table below shows the hours that Mo worked last week.

Monday	09:00 to 12:30	13:30 to 18:00	
Tuesday	09:00 to 12:30	13:30 to 18:00	
Wednesday	09:00 to 12:30	13:30 to 18:00	18:30 to 21:30
Thursday	09:00 to 12:30	13:30 to 18:00	18:30 to 21:30
Friday	09:00 to 12:30	13:30 to 18:00	

His basic hourly rate is £15·60.

Hours worked between 6 pm and 7 am are paid at time and a half.

Calculate his gross pay for last week.

7. Jack is going to a festival in the Czech Republic from his home in Glasgow.

His mum orders the tickets costing 1500 Czech Koruna.

His mum lives in Poland so he must pay her back in Polish Zloty.

Rates of exchange	
Pounds Sterling (£)	Other Currencies
1	30·00 Czech Koruna
1	4·96 Polish Zloty

Calculate how many Polish Zloty he must give to his mum. 2

8. A class of pupils were asked about how they travelled to school on a particular day.

   - $\frac{1}{6}$ of the pupils were driven to school in a car.
   - $\frac{2}{5}$ of the pupils took the bus.
   - The rest of the pupils walked to school.

   Calculate the fraction of pupils who walked to school. 3

9. It takes 5 bakers 3 hours to decorate a tray of cupcakes.

   All the bakers work at the same rate.

   Calculate the time taken for 4 bakers working at this rate to decorate the same number of cupcakes.

   Give your answer in **hours and minutes**. 3

10. Canoeists in Scotland use water level data to decide if there is enough water in a river to canoe down it.

The data for the River Tweed is shown below.

Table 1

Time	Water Level (metres)
Friday 2015	1·55
Friday 2200	1·58
Friday 2315	1·67
Saturday 0015	1·70
Saturday 0100	1·88
Saturday 0300	1·97
Saturday 0415	2·05

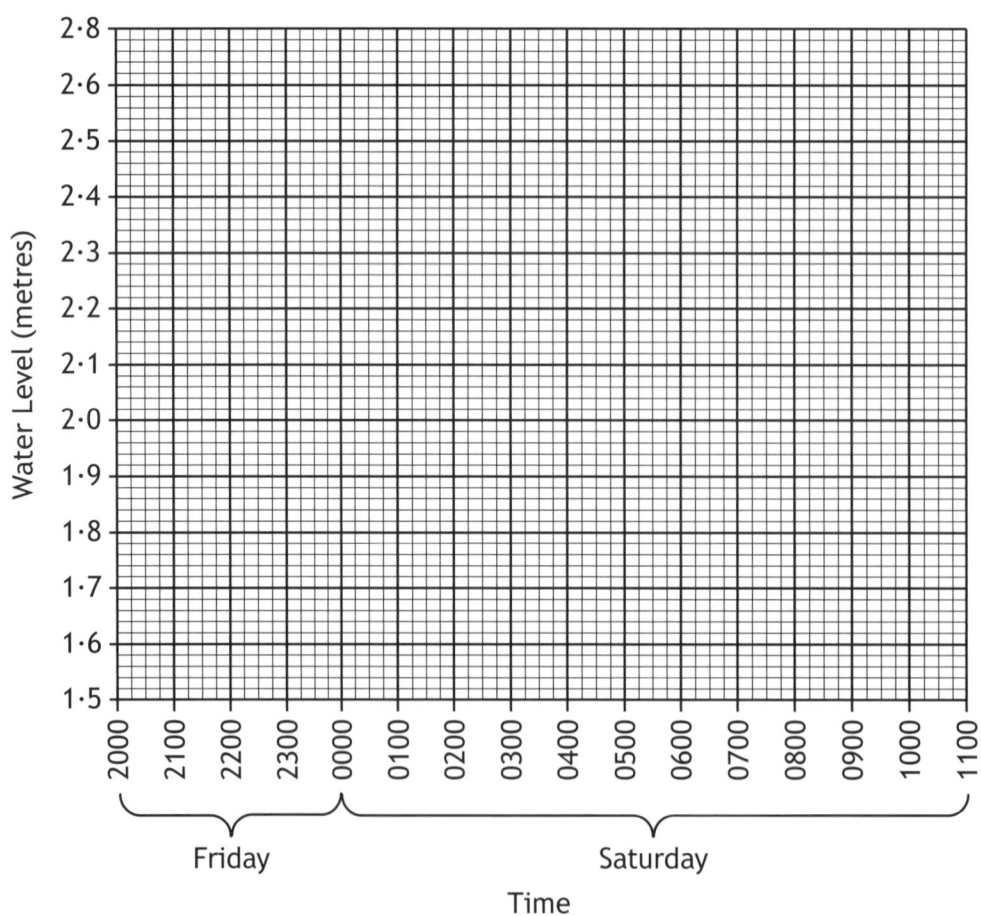

Water Level on River Tweed

(a) (i) Plot the water levels on the scattergraph. **2**

(ii) Draw a line of best fit on the scattergraph. **1**

(An additional graph, if required, can be found on *Page sixteen*.)

10. (continued)

(b) The water level is predicted to rise at the same rate until 1100 on Saturday.

The canoeists use their line of best fit to predict the water level of the River Tweed at 0830 on Saturday.

They hope that it will be "Very High".

Table 2

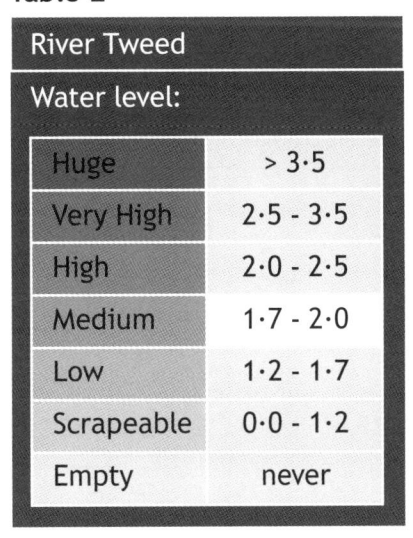

River Tweed	
Water level:	
Huge	> 3·5
Very High	2·5 - 3·5
High	2·0 - 2·5
Medium	1·7 - 2·0
Low	1·2 - 1·7
Scrapeable	0·0 - 1·2
Empty	never

Will the Tweed be "Very High" at 0830?

Justify your answer.

2

11. Mhairi bought 200 shares for £700.

She decides to sell them, but the share price has dropped to £2·75 per share.

She also has to pay a fee of 2½% of her selling price when she sells her shares.

Calculate the loss that she has made. **4**

12. The diagram shows a planned zip line for a play park.

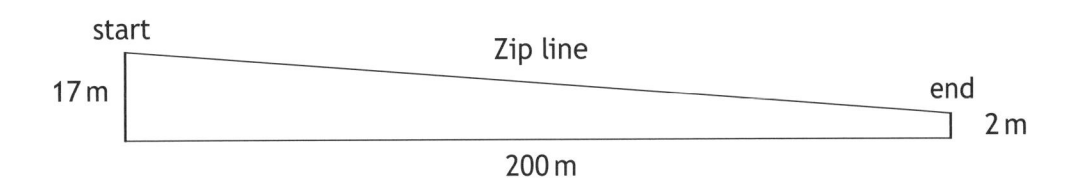

start
17 m
Zip line
end
2 m
200 m

It is recommended that the average gradient of the zip line should be between 0·06 and 0·08 to be safe.

Does the planned zip line meet these safety recommendations?

Use your working to justify your answer. **3**

13. Joe buys a plot of land in the shape of a rectangle and a semi-circle, as shown below.

8 m

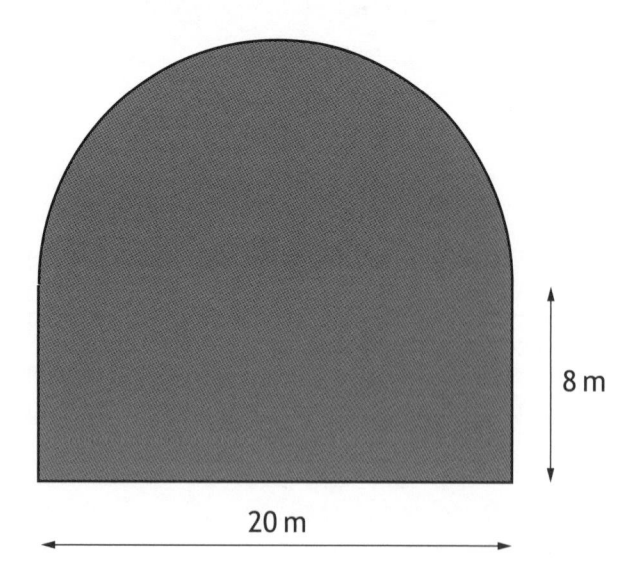

20 m

He plans to put a fence around the plot of land.

He employs Fence Direct to build the fence.

Fence Direct charges £15 per metre including all materials and labour.

(a) Calculate the cost of the fence.

Take $\pi = 3.14$.

3

13. (continued)

   (b) Fence Direct provides a team of workers to build the fence.

   The table shows the list of tasks and the time taken to complete them.

Task	Detail	Preceding Task	Time (hours)
A	Take down old fence	None	2
B	Measure length of fence needed	None	0·5
C	Mark on the ground where new posts must go	None	0·5
D	Collect materials and tools from yard	B	1
E	Hammer posts into the ground	A, C, D	4
F	Attach metal fencing to posts	E	2
G	Attach barbed wire to top of posts	F	1
H	Gather up rubbish	G	2
I	Gather up tools	G	0·5
J	Take rubbish to recycling centre	H	1
K	Put tools back in yard	I	0·5

   Complete the diagram below by writing these tasks and times in the boxes. **2**

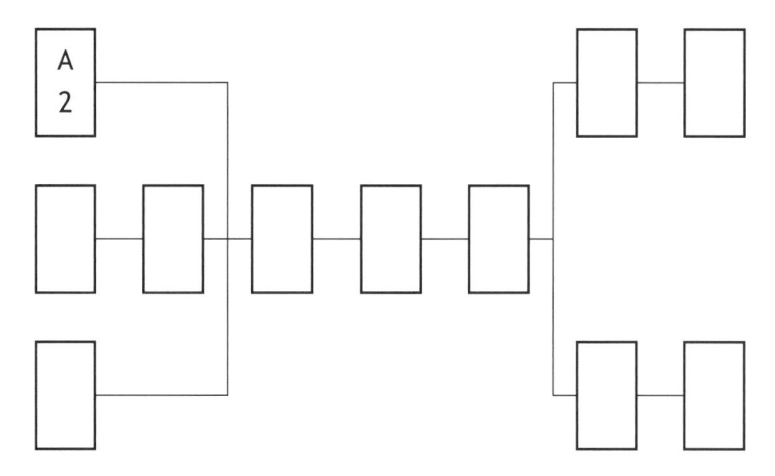

   (An additional diagram, if required, can be found on *Page seventeen*.)

   (c) Fence Direct claims that all of these tasks can be completed in 10 hours.

   Is this a valid claim?

   Use your working to justify your answer. **2**

[END OF SPECIMEN QUESTION PAPER]

Page fifteen

ADDITIONAL SPACE FOR ANSWERS

Additional diagram for Question 5 (c)

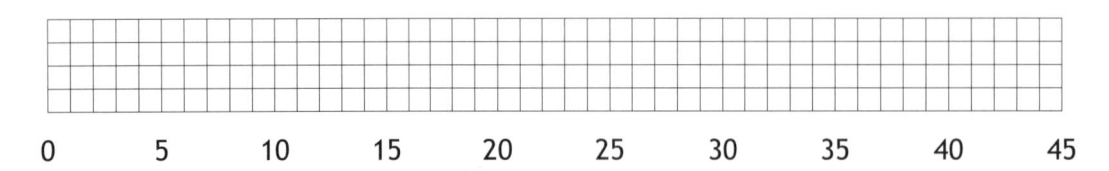

0   5   10   15   20   25   30   35   40   45

Additional graph for Question 10 (a)

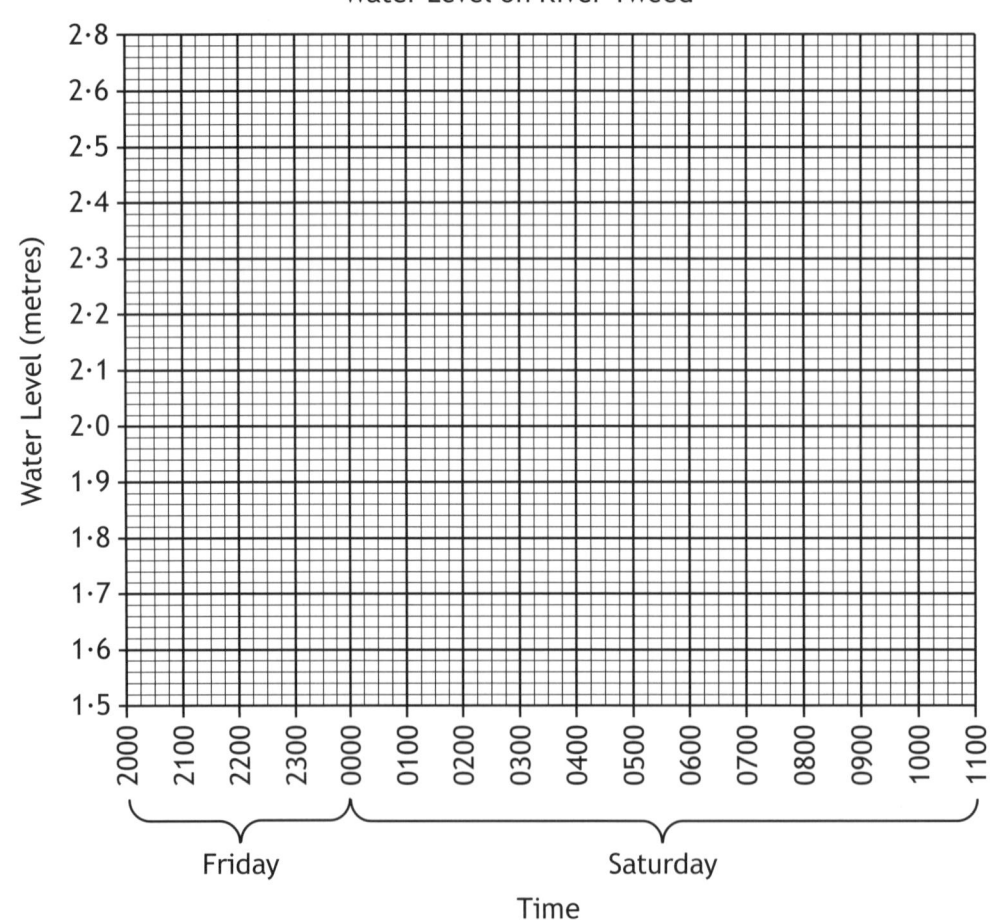

Water Level on River Tweed

Water Level (metres)

Time

Friday   Saturday

ADDITIONAL SPACE FOR ANSWERS

Additional diagram for Question 13 (b)

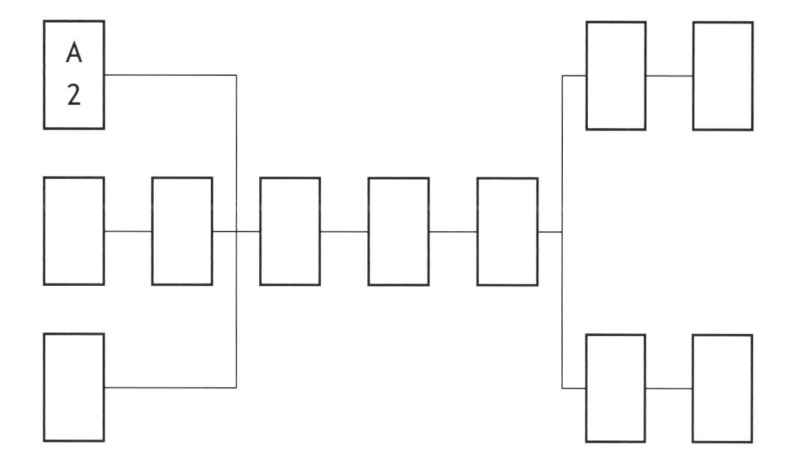

ADDITIONAL SPACE FOR ANSWERS

FOR OFFICIAL USE

N5 National Qualifications SPECIMEN ONLY

Mark

S844/75/02

Applications of Mathematics
Paper 2

Date — Not applicable

Duration — 2 hours

Fill in these boxes and read what is printed below.

Full name of centre

Town

Forename(s)

Surname

Number of seat

Date of birth

Day   Month   Year

Scottish candidate number

Total marks — 65

Attempt ALL questions.

You may use a calculator.

To earn full marks you must show your working in your answers.

State the units for your answer where appropriate.

Write your answers clearly in the spaces provided in this booklet. Additional space for answers is provided at the end of this booklet. If you use this space you must clearly identify the question number you are attempting.

Use **blue** or **black** ink.

Before leaving the examination room you must give this booklet to the Invigilator; if you do not, you may lose all the marks for this paper.

SQA

FORMULAE LIST

Circumference of a circle: $C = \pi d$

Area of a circle: $A = \pi r^2$

Theorem of Pythagoras:

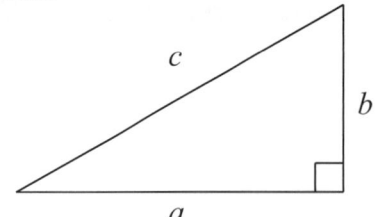

$$a^2 + b^2 = c^2$$

Volume of a cylinder: $V = \pi r^2 h$

Volume of a prism: $V = Ah$

Volume of a cone: $V = \frac{1}{3} \pi r^2 h$

Volume of a sphere: $V = \frac{4}{3} \pi r^3$

Standard deviation: $s = \sqrt{\dfrac{\Sigma(x - \bar{x})^2}{n-1}} = \sqrt{\dfrac{\Sigma x^2 - (\Sigma x)^2 / n}{n-1}}$, where n is the sample size.

Gradient:

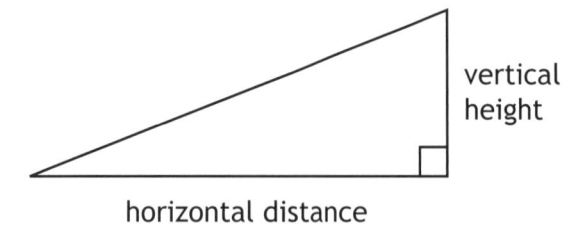

$$\text{gradient} = \frac{\text{vertical height}}{\text{horizontal distance}}$$

Total marks — 65

Attempt ALL questions

1. Erin bought a yacht costing £780 000 in February 2013.

   For the next three years the value of the yacht decreased by 4·1% per annum.

   Calculate the value of the yacht in February 2016.

   Give your answer to **3 significant figures**. 4

2. The fuel tank in Colin's car holds 64 litres of fuel.

Colin started with a full tank and used 40 litres of fuel.

Mark the amount of fuel **remaining** in the tank on the gauge shown below.

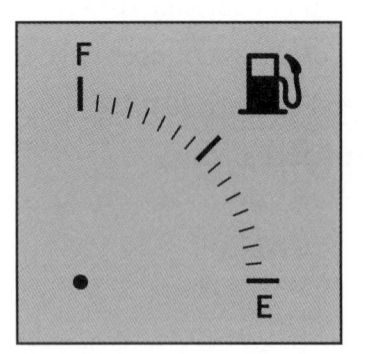

3. An athlete without a coach runs a series of 400 metre races. A sample of his times, in seconds, is shown below.

   47·8   48·3   50·2   49·5   46·9   49·5

   (a) For these times, calculate:

   (i) the mean; **1**

   (ii) the standard deviation. **3**

   (b) The same athlete then decides to train with a coach.

   After training with the coach, the athlete runs a series of races which produces a mean of 49·3 seconds and a standard deviation of 0·23.

   Make two valid comparisons about the times taken by the athlete before and after training with the coach. **2**

4. A garage sells 150 cars in a month.

The bar chart below shows how many cars of each type are sold.

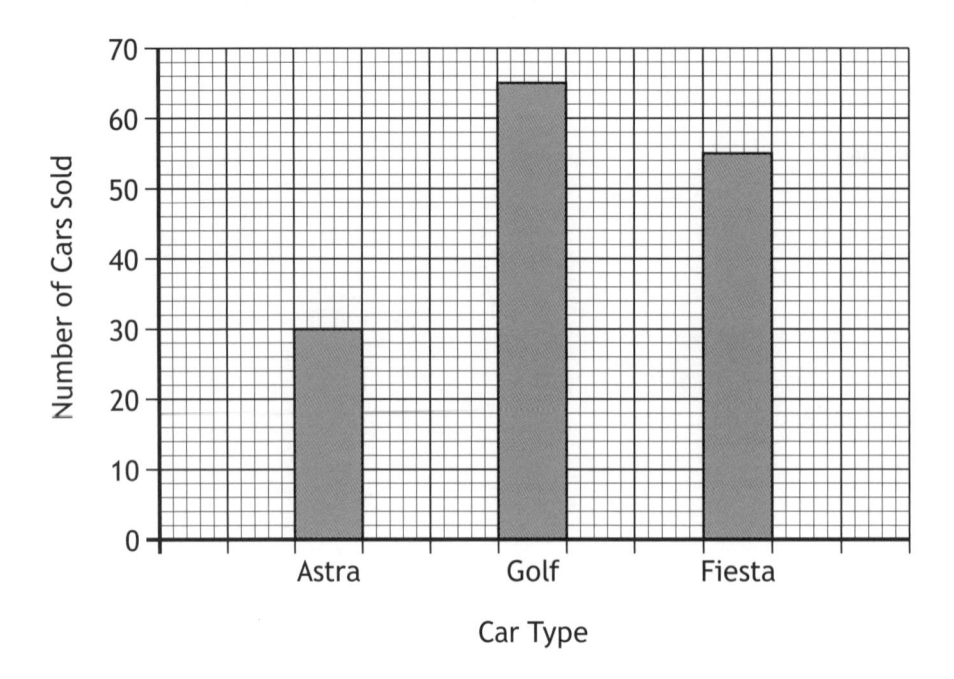

Construct a pie chart to show this information. 3

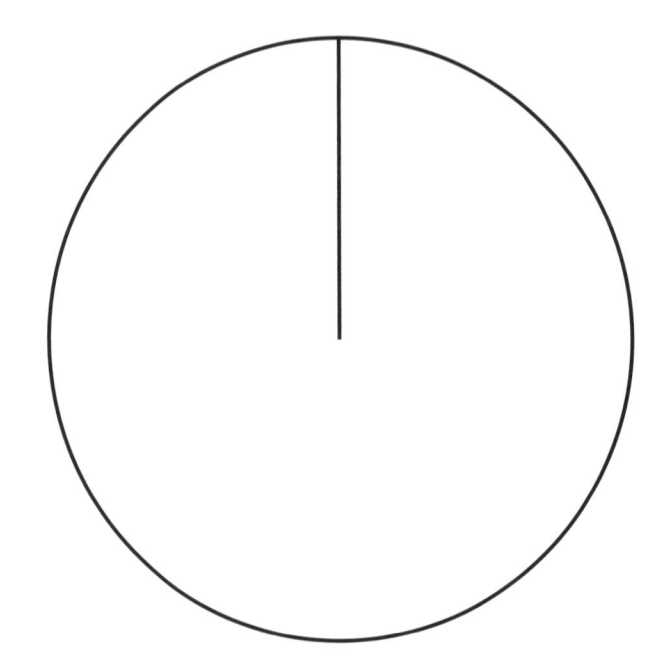

(An additional diagram, if required, can be found on *Page seventeen*.)

5. Donna makes tartan handbags.

   She puts the bags into boxes. The boxes have the dimensions shown below.

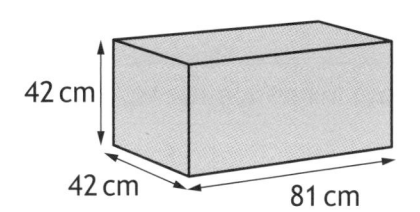

   42 cm, 42 cm, 81 cm

   Donna exports her handbags to the USA in a container. The container has the internal dimensions shown below.

   2·59 m, 2·44 m, 6·06 m

   All the boxes must be aligned in the same direction.

   (a) Calculate the maximum number of boxes that can fit in the container.

   Use your working to justify your answer. **3**

   (b) The rental and shipping of the container costs £1755.

   Each box costs £2·99.

   Each box holds 4 handbags.

   Calculate the cost of shipping per handbag. **2**

6. Graham earns £49 920 per annum.

National Insurance is calculated on a person's salary **before** deductions such as pension contributions.

National Insurance Rates	
Up to £8060	0%
From £8060 to £42 380	12%
Over £42 380	2%

(a) Calculate Graham's annual National Insurance payment. 3

(b) Graham pays 9% of his annual salary into his pension.

Graham's annual income tax is £6870·04.

Graham is paid in 12 monthly payments.

Calculate Graham's monthly net pay. 3

6. (continued)

(c) He wants to buy a new car.

The car loan and running costs would be £460 per month.

He makes a table to show his monthly income and outgoings.

	Income	Outgoings
Take home pay		
Rent		£750
Bills		£450
Food		£625
Entertainment		£125
Child care		£350

Will Graham have enough money each month to get this particular car?
Use your working to justify your answer.

2

7. The boat leaves from the harbour on a bearing of 045° for a distance of 22 miles to Puffin Island.

The boat leaves Puffin Island on a bearing of 170° and travels for a further 37 miles to Gull Isle.

(a) Construct a scale drawing to illustrate this journey.

Use a scale of 1 cm : 5 miles.

(An additional diagram, if required, can be found on *Page eighteen*.)

N

Harbour

The boat continues back to the harbour.

(b) Use the scale drawing to determine the bearing and distance of the harbour from the boat.

7. (continued)

(c) The boat leaves the harbour at 0930.

It stops for 1 hour 15 minutes at Puffin Island and 2 hours 50 minutes at Gull Isle.

The boat arrives back at the harbour at 1800 the same day.

Calculate the average speed of the boat whilst it is moving.

8. Fiona is planning to stay in New York, USA, for three days.
   The table shows the attractions Fiona wants to visit and how much they cost.

Attraction	Full price in US Dollars
Empire State Building	$32
Top of the Rock Observation Deck	$30
Statue of Liberty Cruise	$40
9/11 Memorial and Museum	$24
Waxworks	$37
One World Observatory	$32

   Fiona plans to buy a discount card to reduce the cost of visiting these attractions.

   There are three different discount cards.

   Not all of the attractions are included in all of the cards. Fiona must pay full price for these.

   Card 1: NY Card

   ### NY Card
   Attractions:

   ★ Sea and Space Museum ★   ★ Top of the Rock Observation Deck ★

   ★ Museum of Natural History ★   ★ 9/11 Memorial and Museum ★

   ★ Statue of Liberty Cruise ★   ★ Empire State Building ★

   ★★★★ Total Cost $114 ★★★★

   Benefits:
   > These six attractions can be visited for a single payment of $114.
   > This card can only be used once per attraction.
   > It is valid for 30 days from first use.

   Card 2: Explore NY Card

   ### Explore NY Card
   Attractions:

   9/11 Memorial and Museum • Statue of Liberty Cruise
   Museum of Natural History • Sea and Space Museum
   Empire State Building • Top of the Rock Observation Deck
   Waxworks • Carnegie Hall • Rockefeller Centre Tour

   Cost for any 3 attractions $71

   Benefits:
   > This card can be used for any 3 attractions from the list.
   > This card can only be used once per attraction.
   > It is valid for 30 days from first use.

8. (continued)

Card 3: NY Town Pass

NY Town Pass

80+ attractions are included for one price.
The card is valid for 1, 2, 3 or 5 days.

Cost
$90   1 day pass $180   3 day pass
$140 2 day pass $190   5 day pass

Benefits:
All of Fiona's chosen attractions can be visited with this card.

(a) During her three-day visit, Fiona will visit two attractions each day.

Fiona is going to buy one discount card.

(i) Calculate the total cost of all six attractions if Fiona buys Card 1. **2**

(ii) Calculate the cheapest price that Fiona could pay for entry to her six chosen attractions. **4**

(b) Fiona pays the cheapest price for entry to her six chosen attractions.

She pays before leaving the UK.

The cost is £100·96.

Calculate the exchange rate that Fiona received.

Give your answer correct to **3 decimal places**. **2**

9. A garden in the shape of a **right-angled triangle** has a semi-circular pond on the hypotenuse as shown below.

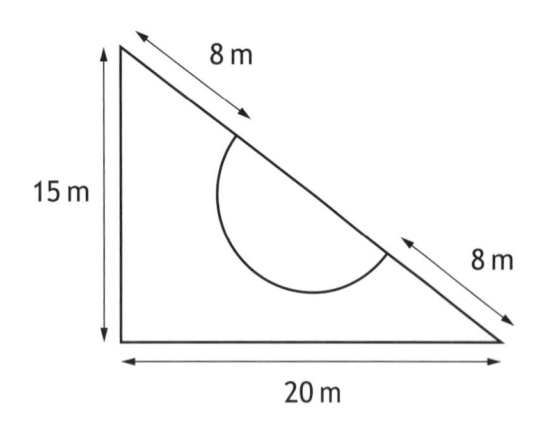

(a) Calculate the diameter of the pond. **2**

(b) The garden, excluding the pond, is to be covered with stone chips.

Calculate the area to be covered with stone chips. **3**

(c) The stone chips come in 25 kg bags costing £2·59 each.

1000 kg of chips covers an area of 20 m².

Calculate the cost of the stone chips for the garden. **3**

10. Brendan makes candles from blocks of wax.

   Each block of wax is a cuboid measuring 30 cm by 20 cm by 20 cm as shown.

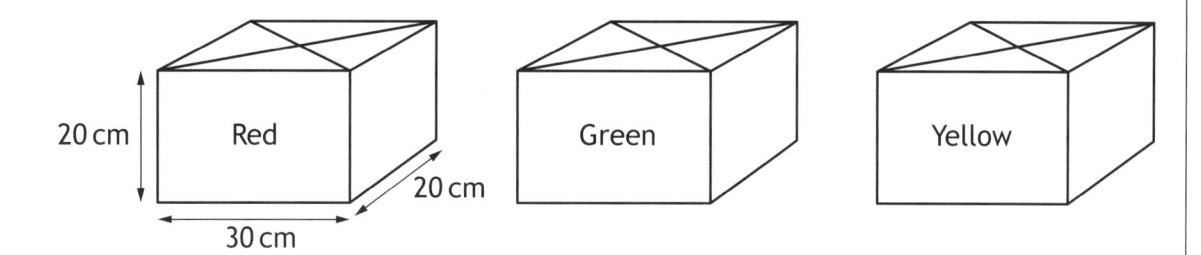

   Each candle contains the colours red, green and yellow in the ratio 3 : 1 : 2 respectively.

   Each candle is a cube with volume 729 cm³.

   (a) Brendan only has 1 block of each colour.

   What is the maximum number of candles that he can make? **3**

   (b) Brendan makes the maximum number of candles.

   Any wax that is left over is thrown away.

   Each block of wax costs £13·75.

   Brendan also buys wicks which cost 18p per candle.

   Brendan adds 65% to his costs when calculating the selling price of each candle.

   What is Brendan's selling price for each candle? **3**

10. (continued)

Brendan also makes blue candles in the shape of a cylinder with a cone on top as shown.

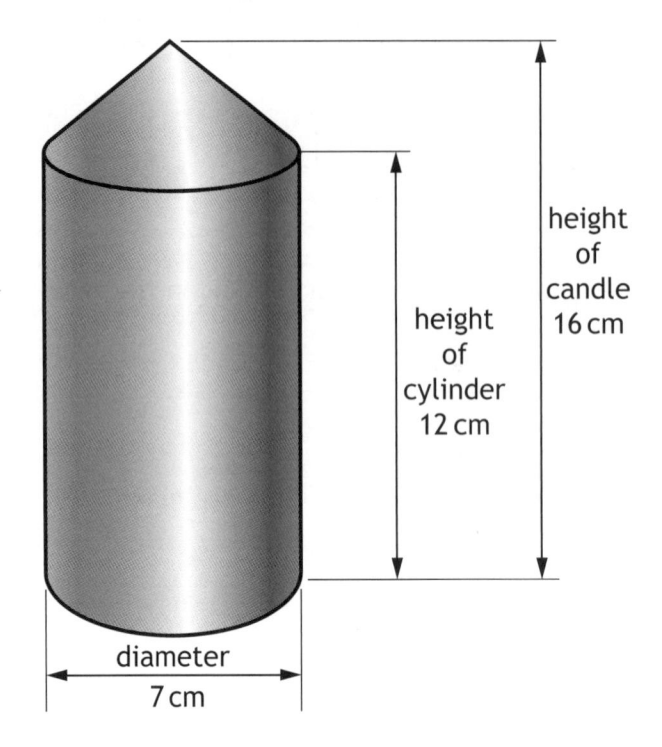

height of cylinder 12 cm
height of candle 16 cm
diameter 7 cm

(c) He buys blue wax in blocks with volume 12 000 cm³.

Brendan thinks that he can make 25 of these candles from one block of wax.

Is he correct?

Use your working to justify your answer. **7**

[END OF SPECIMEN QUESTION PAPER]

ADDITIONAL SPACE FOR ANSWERS

Additional diagram for Question 4

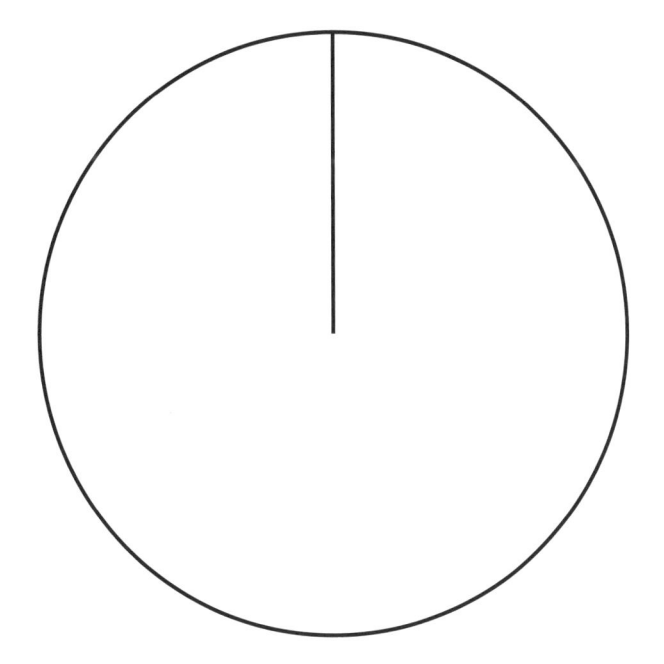

ADDITIONAL SPACE FOR ANSWERS

Additional diagram for Question 7 (a)

ADDITIONAL SPACE FOR ANSWERS

ADDITIONAL SPACE FOR ANSWERS

NATIONAL 5
2018

N5

National Qualifications 2018

Mark

X844/75/01

**Applications of Mathematics
Paper 1 (Non-Calculator)**

THURSDAY, 3 MAY
9:00 AM — 10:05 AM

Fill in these boxes and read what is printed below.

Full name of centre

Town

Forename(s)

Surname

Number of seat

Date of birth
Day Month Year

Scottish candidate number

Total marks — 45

Attempt ALL questions.

You may NOT use a calculator.

To earn full marks you must show your working in your answers.

State the units for your answer where appropriate.

Write your answers clearly in the spaces provided in this booklet. Additional space for answers is provided at the end of this booklet. If you use this space you must clearly identify the question number you are attempting.

Use **blue** or **black** ink.

Before leaving the examination room you must give this booklet to the Invigilator; if you do not, you may lose all the marks for this paper.

SQA

FORMULAE LIST

Circumference of a circle: $C = \pi d$

Area of a circle: $A = \pi r^2$

Theorem of Pythagoras:

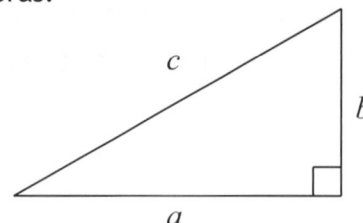

$$a^2 + b^2 = c^2$$

Volume of a cylinder: $V = \pi r^2 h$

Volume of a prism: $V = Ah$

Volume of a cone: $V = \frac{1}{3}\pi r^2 h$

Volume of a sphere: $V = \frac{4}{3}\pi r^3$

Standard deviation: $s = \sqrt{\dfrac{\Sigma(x-\bar{x})^2}{n-1}} = \sqrt{\dfrac{\Sigma x^2 - (\Sigma x)^2/n}{n-1}}$, where n is the sample size.

Gradient:

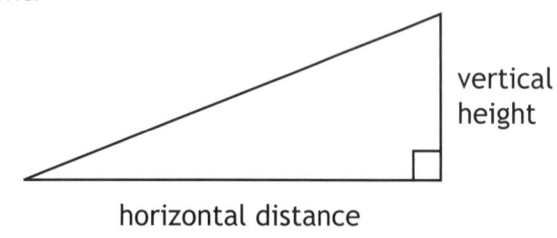

$$\text{gradient} = \frac{\text{vertical height}}{\text{horizontal distance}}$$

Total marks — 45

Attempt ALL questions

1. A baking company will reject cakes if they do not weigh $400\,g \pm 3\%$.

    The weights of a sample of 13 cakes are shown below.

    385, 391, 409, 403, 386, 412, 413, 407, 400, 390, 387, 405, 388

    Calculate the fraction of cakes that will be rejected.

    Use your working to justify your answer.

2. Jennifer is planning to go on a **4 night** city break.

The costs are shown in the table below.

Flights	£270
Accommodation	£90 per night
Spending money	£450
Insurance	£30

She earns £400 per week.

She saves $\frac{1}{8}$ of her earnings each week towards her city break.

Calculate the minimum number of weeks it will take Jennifer to save enough money for her city break.

3. The heights and weights of 8 children aged six are recorded in the table below.

Height in centimetres	104	107	120	124	99	127	104	130
Weight in kilograms	18	19	24	22	17	25	19	24

(a) On the grid below draw a scattergraph to show this data.

(An additional grid, if required, can be found on *Page seventeen*.)

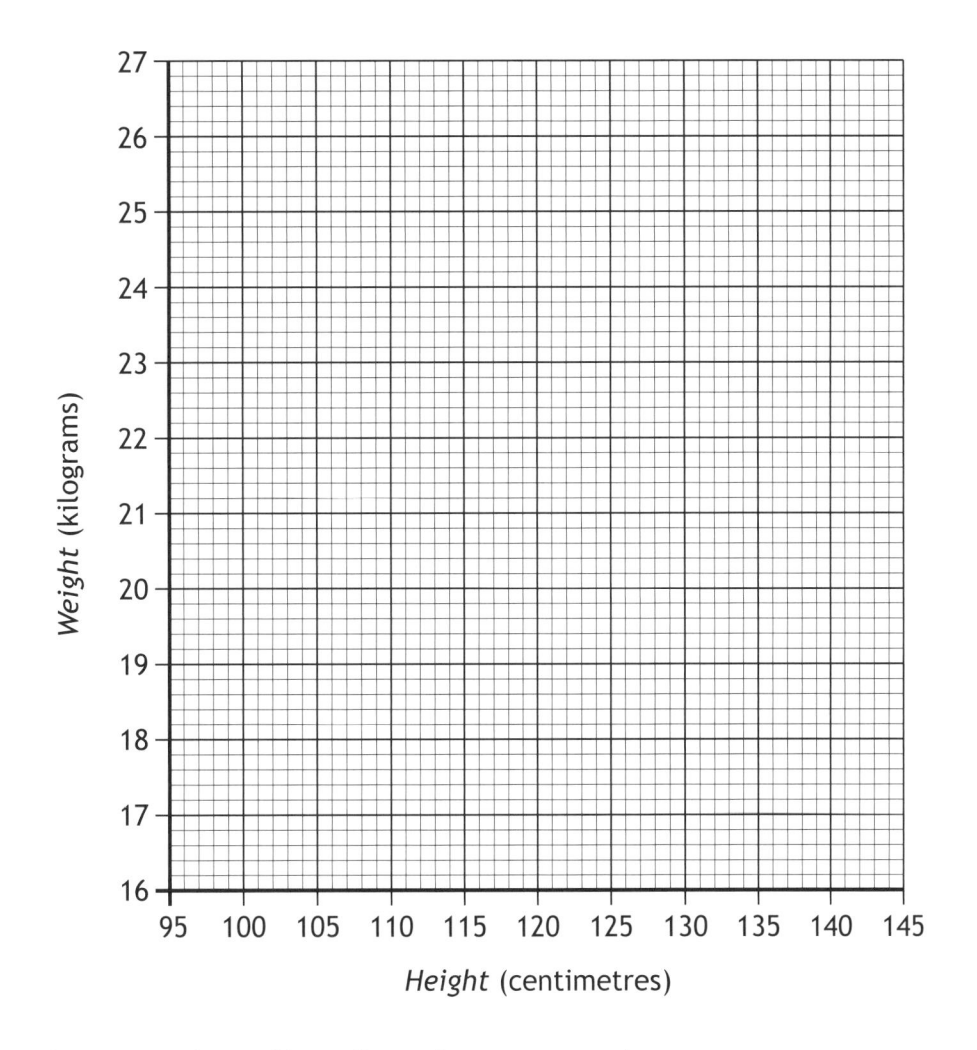

(b) Draw a line of best fit on the scattergraph.

(c) Use your line of best fit to estimate the height of a child who weighs 20 kilograms.

4. Lynn is flying an aircraft and has been told that the outside temperature is 34 °C lower than the ground temperature.

   The ground temperature is 6 °C.

   Calculate the outside temperature and mark it on the gauge below.

   (An additional gauge, if required, can be found on *Page eighteen*.)

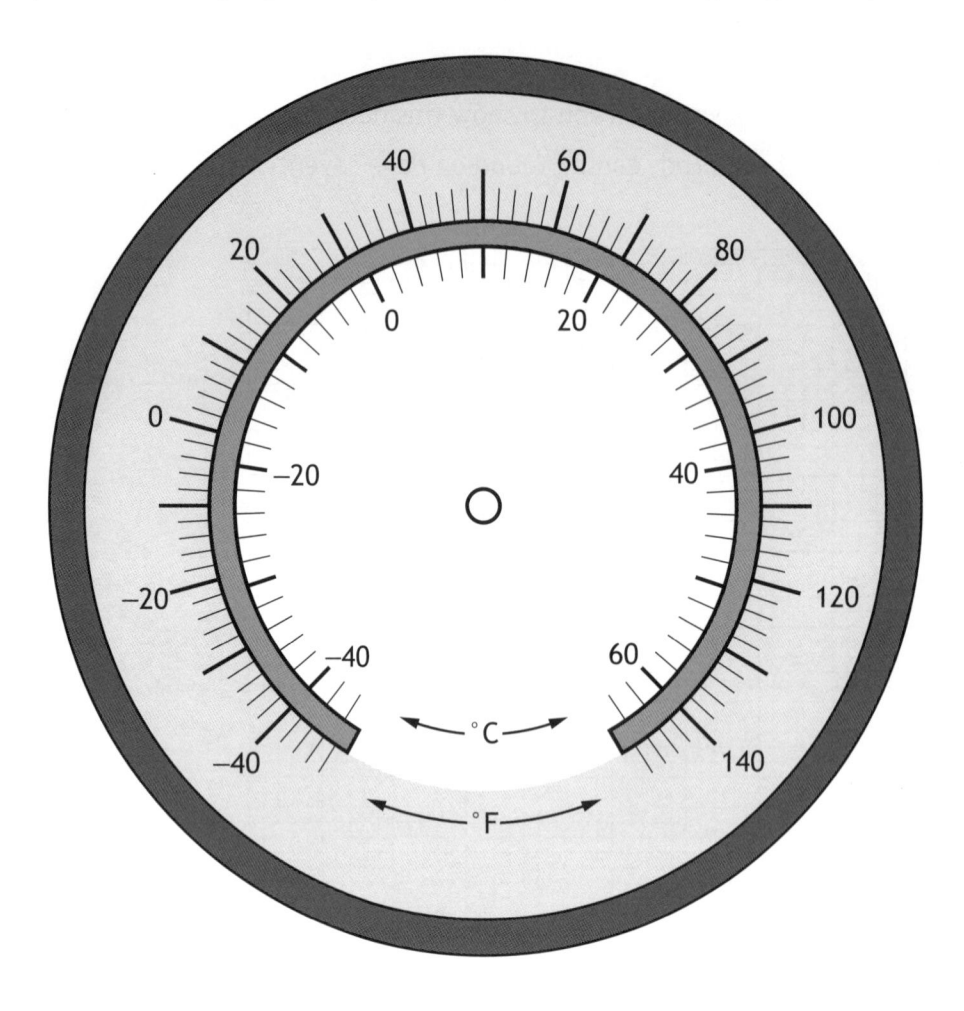

5. Guests at a wedding were asked to choose their main course.

- $\frac{3}{7}$ of the guests chose chicken
- $\frac{1}{3}$ of the guests chose beef
- the remaining guests chose the vegetarian option.

Calculate the fraction of guests that chose the vegetarian option.

3

6. Tom thinks that the answer to the following calculation is 8·7.

$$27·2 - 4·6 \times 3 + 4·7$$

Is Tom correct?
Use your working to justify your answer.

2

7. Gavin is going to South America to do charity work.

   He changes £750 into Bolivian boliviano.

Currency exchange	
Pounds sterling (£)	Other currencies
1	20 Argentine peso
1	9 Bolivian boliviano
1	4 Brazilian real

   (a) How many Bolivian boliviano will he receive? **1**

   He spends 2700 Bolivian boliviano.

   He changes the remaining Bolivian boliviano into Argentine peso.

   (b) How many Argentine peso will he receive? **2**

8. Ian buys a new sofa.

   The original price was £700.

   The shop is having a sale with 25% off the price of all sofas.

   When he goes to the shop he finds there is an additional 5% off the sale price.

   Calculate the price Ian pays for his sofa.   3

9. Steven flew to Hong Kong to start a new job.

The flight included a stop in Doha.

He flew from Edinburgh to Doha then from Doha to Hong Kong.

- The flight from Edinburgh to Doha took 6 hours 35 minutes.
- The flight from Doha to Hong Kong took 7 hours 20 minutes.
- Hong Kong is 8 hours ahead of Edinburgh.

Steven's plane took off from Edinburgh at 9:15 am local time.
It landed in Hong Kong at 8:50 am local time.
How long was the stop in Doha?

10. David sat a class test.

    His results are shown in the table below.

	Marks available	Percentage achieved
Paper 1	35	80%
Paper 2	65	60%

    (a) Calculate the number of **marks** he achieved in paper 1.　　1

    (b) Calculate his overall percentage for this test　　1

11. Ribbon has to be placed around the outside of the love heart cake shown below.

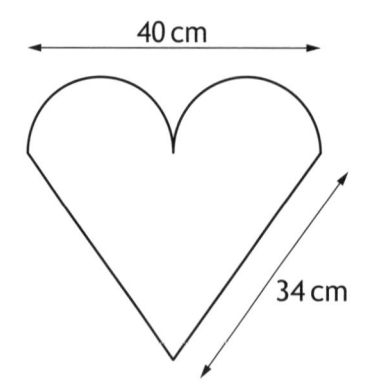

40 cm

34 cm

The top of the cake is in the shape of an isosceles triangle with two identical semi-circles.

The ribbon needs to be the length of the perimeter of the top of the cake plus an extra 2·8 cm.

Calculate the length of ribbon needed for the cake.

Take $\pi = 3\cdot 14$.

3

12. A helicopter flew from Aberdeen airport to transport workers to oil rig 1 and then continued on to oil rig 2.

It flew 82 km on a bearing of 042° to oil rig 1.

It then flew 46 km on a bearing of 194° to oil rig 2.

(a) Construct a scale drawing to illustrate this journey.

Use a scale of 1 cm : 10 km.

(An additional diagram, if required, can be found on *Page nineteen*.)

N

Airport

The helicopter then returns to Aberdeen airport from oil rig 2.

(b) Use the scale drawing to determine the distance and bearing of the airport from oil rig 2.

13. A lawn is to be created in the shape of an isosceles triangle with dimensions as shown below.

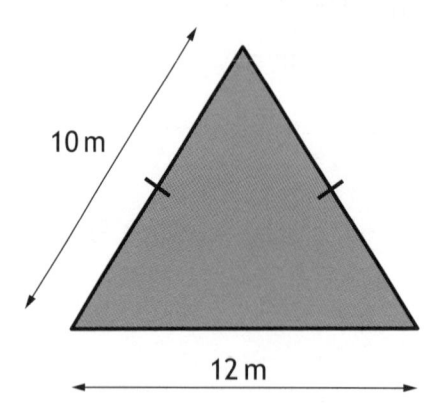

10 m

12 m

Calculate the area of the lawn.

14. Michael runs a stall at the school fayre.

His game requires two spinners to be spun and allowed to come to rest.

The spinners are shown below.

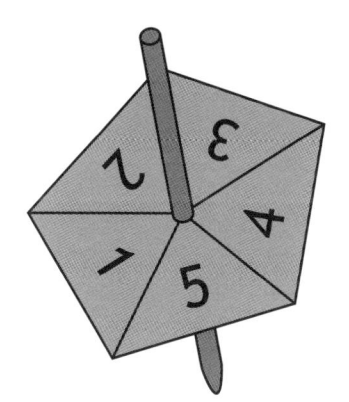

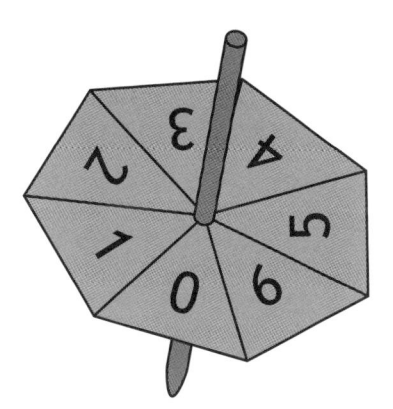

The numbers on which the spinners come to rest are multiplied together.

To win a prize the answer to this multiplication must be **less than 5**.

Calculate the probability of winning a prize.   3

15. A ramp to allow wheelchair access to a school has the dimensions shown below.

Height 25 cm

ramp

Horizontal distance
4 m

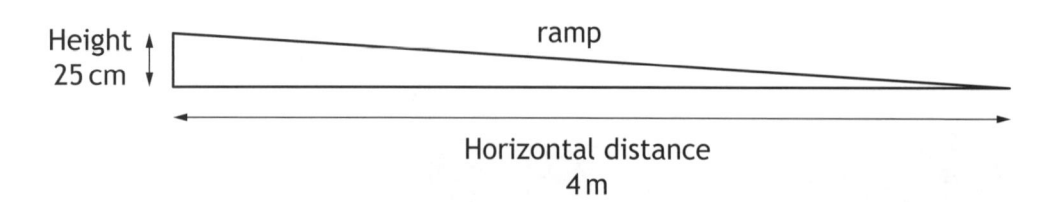

The maximum gradient allowed for a ramp with a horizontal distance of 4 m is $\frac{1}{14}$.

Does the gradient of this ramp meet the regulations?

Use your working to justify your answer. **3**

[END OF QUESTION PAPER]

ADDITIONAL SPACE FOR ANSWERS

Additional grid for use in question 3 (a)

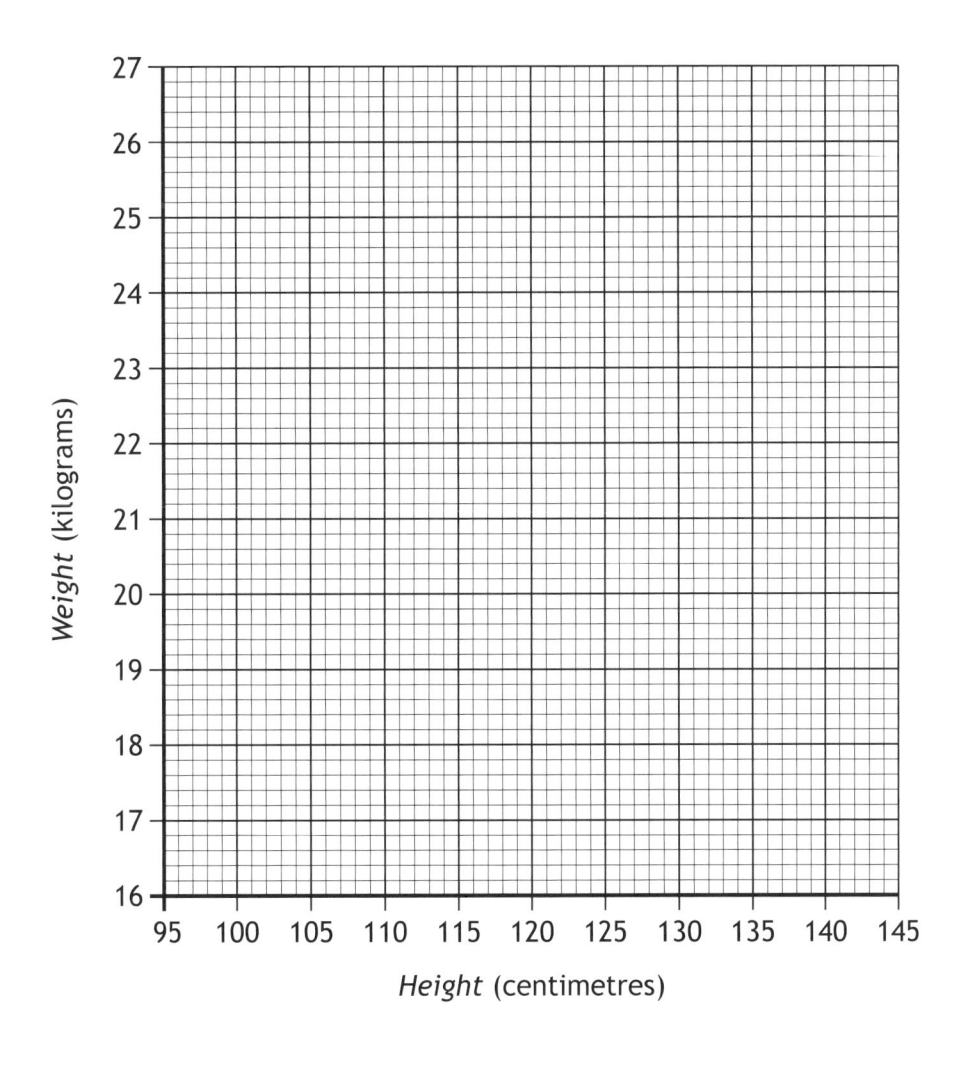

ADDITIONAL SPACE FOR ANSWERS

Additional gauge for use in question 4

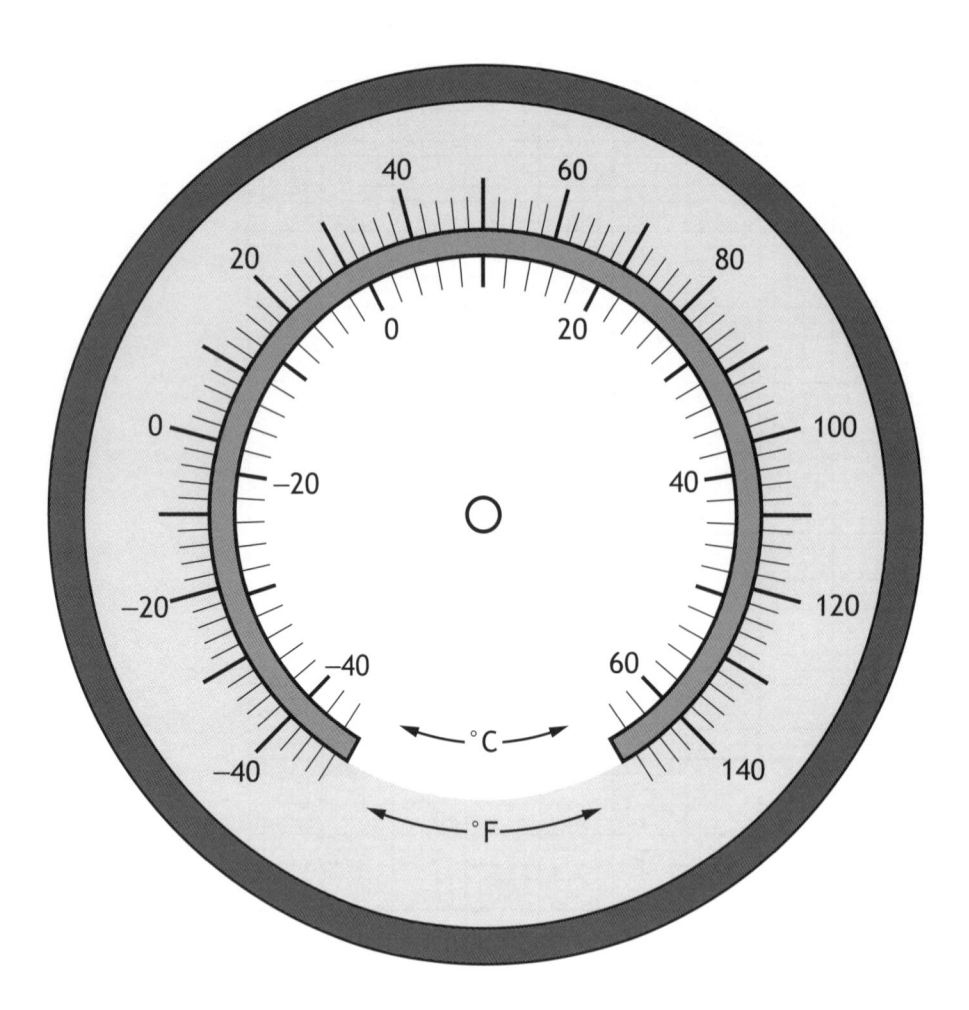

ADDITIONAL SPACE FOR ANSWERS

Additional diagram for use in question 12 (a)

N
↑
|
|
Airport

ADDITIONAL SPACE FOR ANSWERS

ADDITIONAL SPACE FOR ANSWERS

N5

National Qualifications 2018

FOR OFFICIAL USE

Mark

X844/75/02

Applications of Mathematics Paper 2

THURSDAY, 3 MAY
10:25 AM — 12:25 PM

Fill in these boxes and read what is printed below.

Full name of centre

Town

Forename(s)

Surname

Number of seat

Date of birth
Day Month Year

Scottish candidate number

Total marks — 65

Attempt ALL questions.

You may use a calculator.

To earn full marks you must show your working in your answers.

State the units for your answer where appropriate.

Write your answers clearly in the spaces provided in this booklet. Additional space for answers is provided at the end of this booklet. If you use this space you must clearly identify the question number you are attempting.

Use **blue** or **black** ink.

Before leaving the examination room you must give this booklet to the Invigilator; if you do not, you may lose all the marks for this paper.

SQA

FORMULAE LIST

Circumference of a circle: $C = \pi d$

Area of a circle: $A = \pi r^2$

Theorem of Pythagoras:

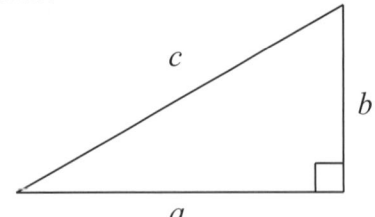

$$a^2 + b^2 = c^2$$

Volume of a cylinder: $V = \pi r^2 h$

Volume of a prism: $V = Ah$

Volume of a cone: $V = \frac{1}{3} \pi r^2 h$

Volume of a sphere: $V = \frac{4}{3} \pi r^3$

Standard deviation: $s = \sqrt{\dfrac{\Sigma(x-\bar{x})^2}{n-1}} = \sqrt{\dfrac{\Sigma x^2 - (\Sigma x)^2 / n}{n-1}}$, where n is the sample size.

Gradient:

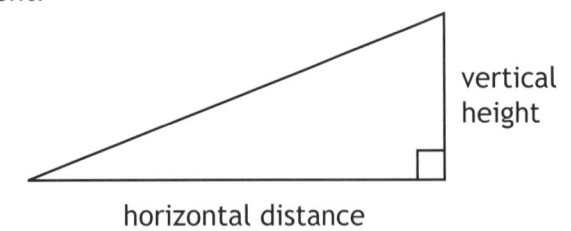

$$\text{gradient} = \frac{\text{vertical height}}{\text{horizontal distance}}$$

Total marks — 65

Attempt ALL questions

1. Jack bought a car 3 years ago costing £1400.

   The car has decreased in value by 13% each year.

   (a) Calculate the current value of the car.

   Give your answer to **2 significant figures**.   4

   Jack sells his car for £950.

   (b) Calculate his loss as a percentage of the **original price**.   2

2. The number of podcasts Omar downloaded each month for a year is shown in the table below.

12	34	19	22	9	13
21	19	5	26	10	28

(a) For this data, calculate:

the median
the lower quartile
the upper quartile. **2**

(b) Construct a boxplot for this data. **2**

(An additional diagram, if required, can be found on *Page twenty-one*.)

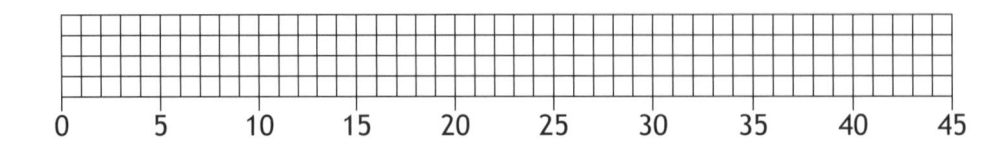

3. Ross is changing his internet package.

The table below shows the internet packages he is considering.

Package	Speed (Mbps)	Usage	Monthly line rental	Monthly broadband cost	Initial fee	Length of contract
A	52	25 GB	£8·95	£19·99	£59·99	12 months
B	52	Unlimited	£8·95	£20·99	£59·99	12 months
C	38	50 GB	£7·99	£16·99	£59·99	12 or 18 months
D	52	Unlimited	£7·99	£18·99	£109·99	12 or 18 months
E	52	50 GB	£6·99	£15·99 for 1st 12 months then £19·99	Free	24 months

Ross requires:
- a minimum speed of 52 Mbps
- at least 50 GB of usage
- a 12 month contract.

Ross will choose the package with the lowest overall **annual** price.

Which package will he choose?

Use your working to justify your answer.

3

4. Nicola has joined a gym.

   The pie chart shows the proportion of time that Nicola will spend on each type of workout exercise.

   Types of workout exercises

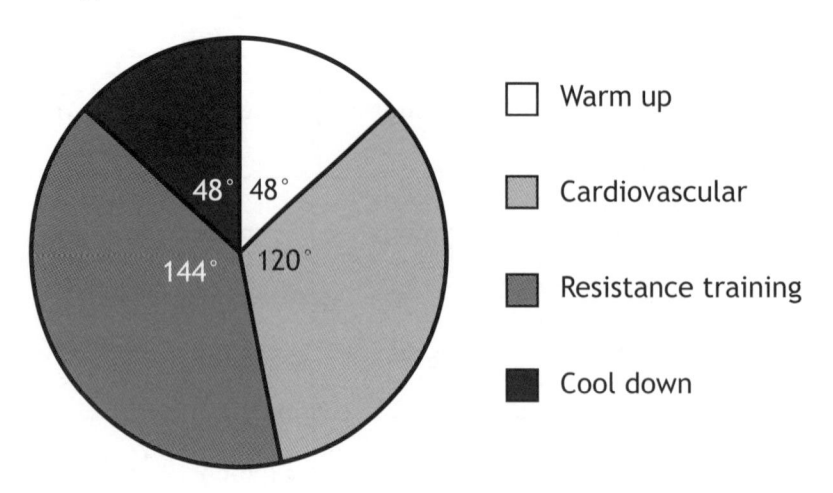

   - Warm up 48°
   - Cardiovascular 120°
   - Resistance training 144°
   - Cool down 48°

   Nicola spent 1 hour and 45 minutes exercising in the gym.

   (a) Calculate how long, **in minutes**, Nicola spent on resistance training. **2**

   Nicola spent 21 minutes exercising on a treadmill.
   Her average speed was 6·6 km/h.

   (b) Calculate the distance she ran on the treadmill. **2**

5. Three tonnes of sheep food will feed 350 sheep for 18 days.

   The number of sheep **increases** by 100.

   (a) How long will the same weight of food now last? 3

   The storage container for the sheep food is in the shape of a cylinder, with dimensions as shown below.

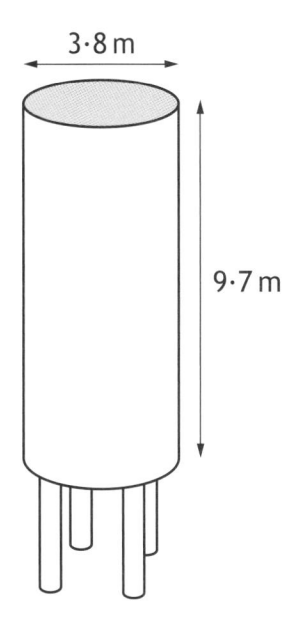

   3·8 m

   9·7 m

   (b) Calculate the volume of the storage container. 2

6. Ali, Kate and Jim are paid to deliver leaflets advertising a new restaurant.

   They shared the money they were paid in a ratio of 3 : 5 : 7.

   Jim received £154.

   Calculate how much the restaurant paid, **in total**, to deliver the leaflets.

7. Sam drives from Paris in France to Zurich in Switzerland.

   He knows:
   - his car will cover an average of 47 miles per gallon of fuel
   - the fuel tank holds 50 litres of fuel when it is full
   - it is 650 km from Paris to Zurich.

   Will Sam be able to complete his journey with one full tank of fuel?

   Use your working to justify your answer.

   1 mile = 1·609 km
   1 gallon = 4·545 litres

8. Scott decides to build a new track bike.

   Scott needs to buy a frame, a handlebar, a pair of pedals, a saddle, 2 wheels and 2 tyres.

   Different retailers offer these parts.

   The prices, in pounds, are shown in the table.

Retailer	Handlebar	Pedals (pair)	Wheels (each)	Saddle	Tyres (each)
Bikes 2 Go	63·33	33·33	51·25	41·66	54·98
Bikevelo	55·49	42·50	46·66	62·37	58·33
Velo cycles	68·83	36·66	61·20	53·99	61·66
Cycle trax	59·50	43·33	52·25	63·33	69·99
EP bikes	71·58	41·66	44·49	47·85	49·99

   Scott can buy the parts from different retailers.

   The bike frame costs £2640·95.

   (a) Calculate the **minimum** total cost of the frame and parts. 2

8. (continued)

Scott cannot afford to pay for the bike all at once.

The cash price of the complete bike from EP bikes is £2991·00.

He chooses to buy the complete bike from EP bikes, as they are the only retailer offering a finance package.

The finance package consists of:
- a deposit of 15% of the cash price
- 36 payments of £76·50.

(b) Calculate how much more this finance package will cost compared to the **minimum** total cost. 4

8. (continued)

Scott trains at the velodrome on his new bike.

He records his top speed, in kilometres per hour, for each lap.

Six of these speeds are shown below.

    61·2   58·3   59·1   58·8   60·4   59·8

(c) For these speeds, calculate:

    (i) the mean; **1**

    (ii) the standard deviation. **3**

Scott had a mean top speed on his old bike of 57·3 km/h and a standard deviation of 1·21 km/h.

(d) Make two valid comments comparing his top speed on the two different bikes. **2**

9. A factory produces cans of tinned beans.

The table shows the list of tasks and the time taken to complete them.

Task	Detail	Preceding task	Time (seconds)
A	Boil beans to cook them	C	500
B	Put on lid	H,E	3
C	Blanch dried beans in water	None	300
D	Attach label	I	5
E	Put sauce in tin	F	2
F	Make the sauce	None	900
G	Put in box	D	5
H	Put beans in tin	A	2
I	Cook beans in sauce in tin	B	300

(a) Complete the diagram below to show the tasks and times in the boxes. 1

(An additional diagram, if required, can be found on *Page twenty-one*.)

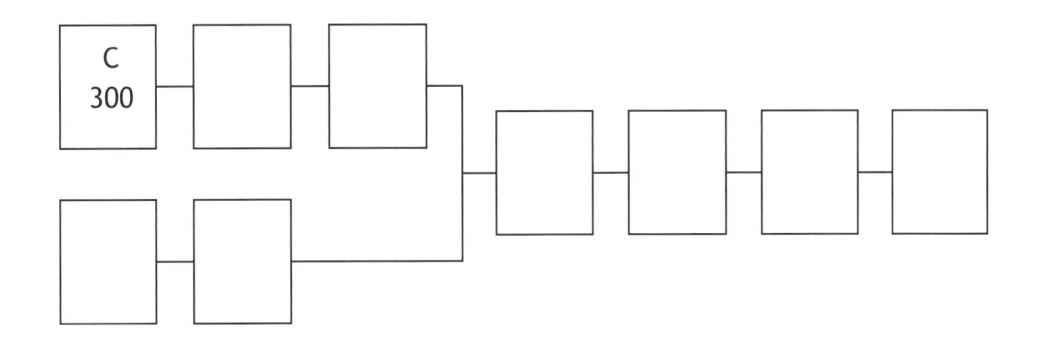

[Diagram: First box shows C, 300. Remaining boxes to be completed.]

The factory manager thinks that the whole process can be completed in less than 25 minutes.

(b) Based on the times given, is the factory manager correct?

Use your working to justify your answer. 2

9. (continued)

The tins are packed in boxes.

Each box has dimensions 60 cm × 40 cm × 15 cm as shown below.

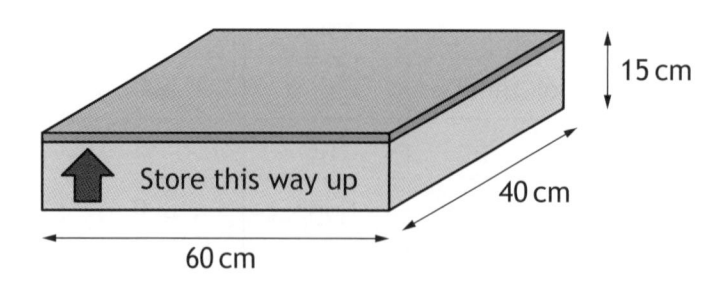

The boxes must be packed into containers for shipping to Canada.

The container has the internal dimensions shown below.

All the boxes must be aligned in the same direction.

(c) Calculate the maximum number of boxes that will fit in the container. 3

9. (continued)

It takes 277 hours to sail from the UK to Canada.

The local time in Canada is 5 hours behind the local time in the UK.

The ship leaves the UK at 2200 on 3rd June.

(d) Calculate the date and local time that the ship will arrive in Canada. **3**

10. Fiona is a vet.

She has started a new job.

Her new salary is £42 000.

National Insurance is calculated on a person's salary **before** deductions such as pension contributions.

National Insurance rates	
Up to £8164	0%
From £8164 to £45 032	12%
Over £45 032	2%

(a) (i) Calculate Fiona's annual National Insurance payment.   2

Fiona's annual income tax payment is £5427·96.

She pays an annual contribution of £3360 into her pension.

Fiona is paid in 12 equal monthly payments.

(ii) Calculate Fiona's monthly net pay.   2

10. (continued)

Fiona plans to rent accommodation.

She needs to work out how much she can afford to spend on rent, electricity and council tax.

The table shows her monthly outgoings.

	Outgoings
Car payment	395
Car insurance	28
Road tax	12
Food	380
Clothes	130
Mobile phone	64
Internet	55
Socialising	250
Loan	200
Savings	200
Total	

(b) Calculate how much she will have available per month for rent, electricity and council tax.

10. (continued)

Fiona is considering these 3 properties.

2 Bedroom House

Total Monthly Cost £730 including Rent, Council Tax and Electricity

1 Bedroom Apartment

Weekly Rent £132
Council Tax Band F
Weekly Electricity £12

3 Bedroom Farmhouse

Monthly Rent £390
Council Tax Band E
Monthly Electricity £76

Annual Council Tax
(to be paid in 12 equal monthly instalments)
Band A: £1000·92
Band B: £1167·72
Band C: £1334·52
Band D: £1501·32
Band E: £1834·92
Band F: £2168·64
Band G: £2502·24
Band H: £3002·64

(c) Which property is the cheapest option?
Use your working to justify your answer.   3

11. A new hotel is being planned in Benidorm.

The pool will have a walkway around three sides.

The walkway will be 1·5 m wide.

This is shown in the diagram.

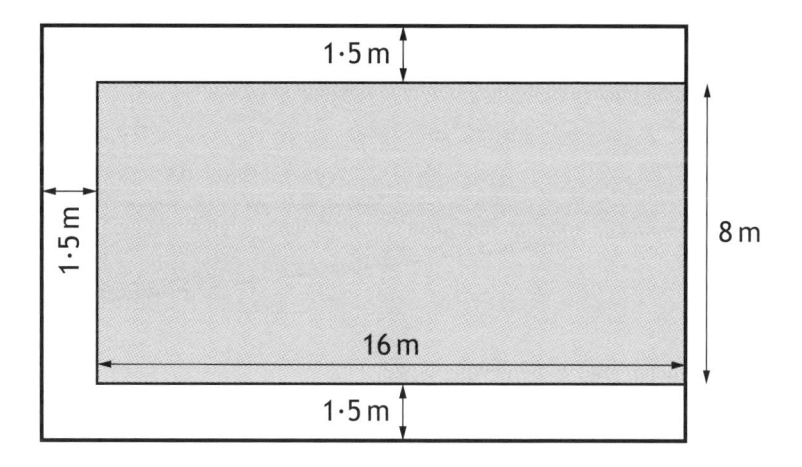

(a) Calculate the total area of the walkway. **2**

The walkway will be covered in tiles.

16 tiles are needed to cover 1 square metre.

The tiles are sold in boxes of 50.

Each box costs 71·95 euro.

(b) Calculate the cost of the tiles needed for the walkway. **2**

11. (continued)

The swimming pool is a prism, with dimensions as shown in the diagram below.

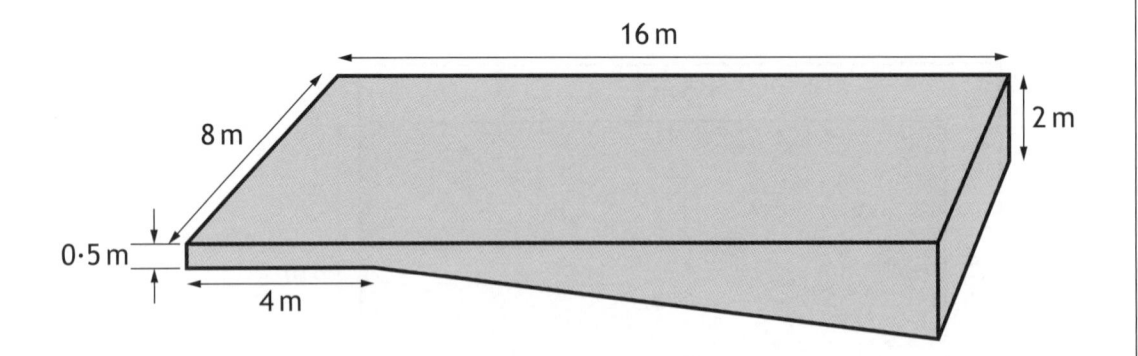

(c) Calculate the volume of the swimming pool.

Give your answer **in litres**. 4

[END OF QUESTION PAPER]

ADDITIONAL SPACE FOR ANSWERS

Additional diagram for use in question 2 (b)

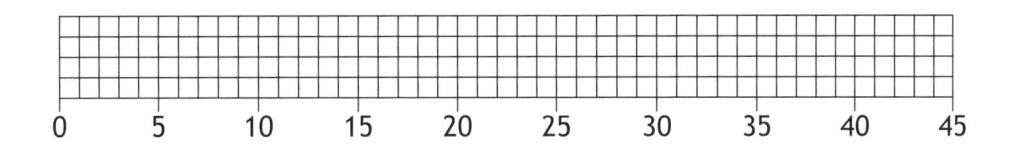

0   5   10   15   20   25   30   35   40   45

Additional diagram for use in question 9 (a)

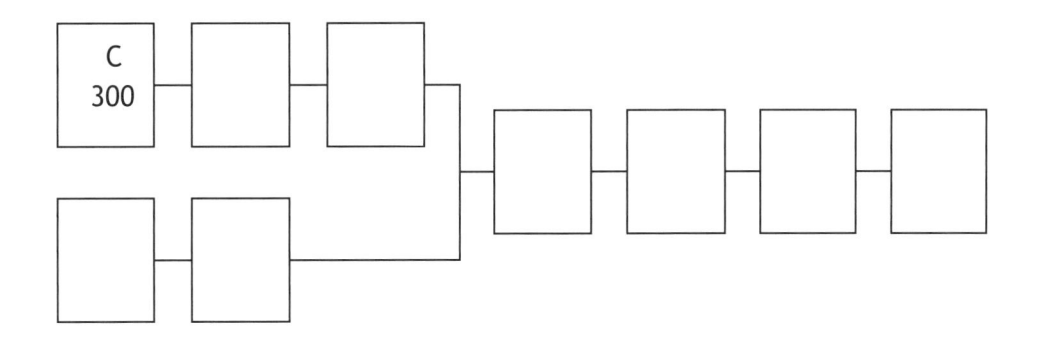

C
300

ADDITIONAL SPACE FOR ANSWERS

ADDITIONAL SPACE FOR ANSWERS

NATIONAL 5
Answers

ANSWERS FOR

SQA NATIONAL 5
APPLICATIONS OF MATHEMATICS 2018

NATIONAL 5 LIFESKILLS MATHEMATICS 2017

One mark is available for each •. There are no half marks.

Paper 1

1. • (194 − 2) × 50
   • 9600 (mm)

2. (a) • Strategy: know how to calculate 2·5% of £6000
      • Calculate 2·5% of £6000: 150
      • Add commission to basic salary: (£)2600
   (b) • Strategy: attempt to calculate gross pay − total deductions
      • (£)1870·39

3. (a) • Communication: 4 points correct
      • Communication: all 6 points correct

D	0	60	120	160	200	260
W	40	110	130	175	220	275

   (b) Line of best fit
   (c) Answer consistent with line of best fit (days)

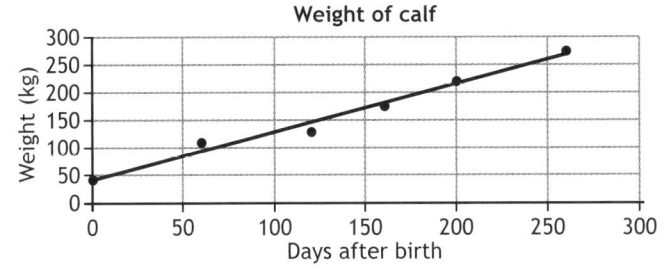

4. • 1·6/8
   • 4/20 (3/20 does not need to be explicitly stated) or 8/40 and 6/40 or 0·2 and 0·15 or equivalent
   • No, supported by working

5. (a) 10 × 14 + 1 = 141, she needs bands D and A
   (b) • Calculate cost for shop 1: 49·50
      • Calculate cost for shop 2: 45·48
      • Conclusion consistent with working: Shop 2
      OR
      • Calculate discount for 1 shop: 26·30 or 30·32 or 27·81
      • Calculate discount for remaining two shops
      • Conclusion consistent with working: Shop 2

6. • Calculate one (£1) share: 2 794 000 ÷ 8 = 349 250
   • Calculate total number of shares: 2·50 + 2·00 + 4·00 + 0·50 = 9
   • Calculate the total amount: 9 × 698 500 = (£)6 286 500
   OR
   • Calculate one (50p) share: 2 794 000 ÷ 8 = 349 250
   • Calculate total number of shares: 1 + 4 + 5 + 8 = 18
   • Calculate total amount: 18 × 349 250 = (£)6 286 500

   OR
   • Calculate the amount for any teacher other than Mr Young: Miss Smith 1 397 000 or Mr Jones 349 250 or Mr Ross 1 746 250
   • Calculate the amount for another teacher: either of the remaining two
   • Calculate amount for final teacher and total amount: 1 397 000 + 349 250 + 1 746 250 + 2 794 000 = 6 286 500

7. (a) • Strategy: know how to calculate composite area
      • 20 (cm^2)
   (b) • Calculate the number of badges per pack: 180 ÷ 20 = 9
      • Calculate the cost of enamel for one badge: 90 ÷ 9 = 10
      • Calculate selling price: 10 + 3 + 17 = (£)30
      OR
      • Calculate the number of badges per pack: 180 ÷ 20 = 9
      • Calculate the total cost of 9 badges: 9 × 3 + 9 × 17 + 90 = 270
      • Calculate selling price: 270 ÷ 9 = (£)30

8. • Identify the blood groups that B+ can help: e.g. AB+ and B+
   • Interpret stacked bar chart: 3 people AB+ and 9 people B+
   • Calculate fraction: $\frac{3+9}{100} = \frac{12}{100} \left(= \frac{3}{25}\right)$

9. (a) • Correct substitution in Pythagoras' Theorem: e.g. $10^2 - 6^2$
      • Calculate the missing side: x = 8
      • Calculate the length of the semi-circle: 3·14 × 6 ÷ 2 = 9·42
      • Calculate the perimeter of the shape: 10 + 8 + 9·42 = 27·42(cm)
   (b) • Strategy: know how to calculate area of rectangular strip
      • (27·42 − 0·3) × $\frac{1}{2}$ = 13·56

Paper 2

1. • Strategy: know how to calculate the volume of half a cylinder
   • $\frac{1}{2} \times \pi \times 7^2 \times 30$
   • 2309·07…cm^3
   OR
   • Strategy: know to calculate the area of the semi-circle and multiply it by 30
   • $\frac{1}{2} \times \pi \times 7^2$
   • = 76·96… × 30 = 2309·07… cm^3

2. (a) • Work out the cost of 8000 shares: 8000 × 0·73 = 5840
      • Calculate percentage decrease: evidence of 0·97
      • Calculate percentage increase: evidence of 1·042
      • Identify power: …^{2}
      • Calculate the value of the shares: (£)6150·64

OR
- Calculate percentage decrease: evidence of 0·97
- Calculate percentage increase: evidence of 1·042
- Identify power: ...²
- Calculate the value of 1 share: 0·768...
- Calculate the value of 8000 shares: (£)6150·64

(b)
- Calculate $\frac{5}{8}$ of 6560 and subtract commission
- Calculate amount received: (£)4087·05

3.
- Calculate new price: 1260 + 151·20 = 1411·20
- Calculate the deposit: $\frac{1}{3}$ of 14 11·20 = 470·40
- Calculate the amount still payable:
  470·40 + 200 = 670·40
  1411·20 − 670·40 = 740·80
- State how much each monthly payment is:
  740·80 ÷ 8 = (£)92·60

4. (a) 71

(b)
- Calculate either median: 61 or 71
- Calculate other median and difference: 71 − 61 = 10

(c)
- Calculate lower quartile: Q_1 = 67
- Calculate upper quartile: Q_3 = 84
- Correct end points drawn: 59 and 95
- Consistent box drawn: box showing Q_1, Q_2 and Q_3

5. (a)
- Calculate the distance from a scale drawing:
  8 × 3000000 = 24000000
- Give answer in kilometres:
  24000000 ÷ 100 ÷ 1000 = 240(km)

(b)
- Calculate average speed and change hours and minutes to hours: $\frac{240}{7.5}$ = ...
- Convert average speed into knots: ... × 0·54 = ...
- Calculate average speed to 2 significant figures:
  17·28 = 17 (2 sig fig)

(c)
- know how to calculate amount of euro: 55% of 2400 × 1·15 ...
- calculate remaining euro: 1518 − 1379 = 139 (euro)

(d) (i)
- state probability $\frac{7}{32}$

(ii)
- calculate denominator of 28
- state probability $\frac{1}{28}$

6. (a)
- Strategy: know to calculate two arrangements
- Calculate one arrangement:
  2·25 m ÷ 0·75 = 3 cages
  15 m ÷ 0·85 = 17 cages
  Total = 3 × 17 × 2 = 102 cages
- Calculate second arrangement and make consistent conclusion:
  2·25 m ÷ 0·85 = 2 cages
  15 m ÷ 0·75 = 20 cages exactly
  Total = 20 × 2 × 2 = 80

(b)
- Calculate basic pay: $1\frac{1}{2}$ × 14·40 = 21·60
- Calculate overtime pay: $8\frac{1}{2}$ × 14·40 × 1·5 = 183·60
- Calculate weekly gross pay: (183·60 + 21·60) × 5
  = 205·20 × 5
  = (£)1026

OR
- Calculate 10 hours basic pay: 10 × 14·40 = 144
- Calculate $8\frac{1}{2}$ hours at $\frac{1}{2}$ time: $8\frac{1}{2}$ × 7·20 = 61·20
- Calculate weekly gross pay:
  (144 + 61·20) × 5 = (£)1026

7. (a) (i)
- (24 + 22 + 19 + 18 + 17 + 17) ÷ 6 = 19·5(°)

(ii)
- Calculate $(x - \bar{x})^2$: 20·25, 6·25, 0·25, 2·25, 6·25, 6·25
- Substitute into formula: $\sqrt{(41.5 \div 5)}$
- Calculate standard deviation: 2·88

(b) Two valid comments
- 1 mark for comment regarding mean, e.g. on average Durban's temperatures are higher
- 1 mark for comment regarding standard deviation, e.g. Durban's temperatures are less consistent

(c)
- Strategy/process: calculate one local time
- Calculate the other two local times: Mumbai 9:00 pm
  London: 1:30 pm
  New York: 8:30 am
- State offices that can take part: New York and London

OR
- Strategy/process: calculate one time difference
- Calculate remaining two time differences:
  Mumbai + 5 h 30 mins
  London −2 h
  New York −7 h
- State offices that can take part: New York and London

OR
- Calculate how long until 3:30 pm: 22 hours 5 minutes
- Calculate local times: Mumbai 9:00 pm
  London: 1:30 pm
  New York: 8:30 am
- State offices that can take part: New York and London

8. (a)
- Calculate short sides of triangle: 500
- Show evidence of the correct form of Pythagoras' theorem: 500² + 500²
- Calculate length of hypotenuse of triangle:
  707·1068... = 707 (mm)

(b)
- Calculate the area of the square encasing pentagonal shower base and subtract area of missing triangle: $900^2 - \frac{1}{2} \times 500 \times 500$
- Calculate area of pentagonal base:
  810000 − 125000 = 685000 (mm²)

(c)
- Strategy: evidence of quarter circle added to rectangles
- Calculate the area of the quarter circle:
  $\frac{1}{4} \times \pi \times 600 \times 600 = 282743$
- 282743 + 450000 = 732743
- Zuzanna should pick the offset quadrant (since 732743 mm² > 685000 mm²)

ANSWERS FOR NATIONAL 5 APPLICATIONS OF MATHEMATICS

OR
- Strategy: evidence of whole square minus area that is not part of the base.
- Calculate the area of the quarter circle:
  $\frac{1}{4} \times \pi \times 600 \times 600 = 282743$
- $810000 - (360000 - 282743) = 732743$
- Zuzanna should pick the offset quadrant (since 732743 mm² > 685000 mm²)

NATIONAL 5 APPLICATIONS OF MATHEMATICS 2017 SPECIMEN QUESTION PAPER

One mark is available for each •. There are no half marks.

Paper 1

1. • Strategy: Add flight time and time zone
   - 7:30 pm

2. • Identify correct values 9 and 66
   - $\frac{3}{22}$

3. • Strategy: know to use upper/lower limits
   - $\frac{17}{20} = 85\%$
   - No, as 85% < 88%

   OR
   - Strategy: know to use upper/lower limits
   - $\frac{3}{20} = 15\%$
   - No, as 15% > 12%

   OR
   - Strategy: know to use upper/lower limits
   - 88% of 20 = 17·6, ie need 18
   - No, as only 17 in tolerance, so batch fails

4. Ans: (£)7·26
   - Strategy: pick correct band F
   - 76·13 and 145
   - 2 × 76·13 − 145 = 7·26

5. (a) • Boys, with valid reason
   (b) • State the median: 26
   - State the quartiles: 18, 30
   (c) [box plot: 10 18 26 30 42]
   - Strategy: end points at 10 and 42
   - Strategy: box showing Q_1, Q_2, Q_3

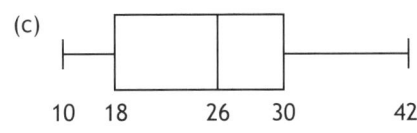

6. • Calculate basic and overtime hours: 40 and 6
   - Calculate overtime: 6 × 1·5 × 15·60 = 140·40
   - Calculate gross weekly pay: 15·60 × 40 + 140·40 = (£)764·40

7. • Strategy: know to divide by 30 then multiply by 4·96
   - 1500 ÷ 30 = 50
   - 50 × 4·96 = 248 (Zloty)

8. • Strategy: know to add fractions
   - $\frac{1}{6} + \frac{2}{5} = \frac{5}{30} + \frac{12}{30} = \frac{17}{30}$
   - $\frac{13}{30}$ or equivalent

9. • Strategy: know how to find the time for 4 bakers
   - 3 × 5 ÷ 4 = 3·75
   - 3 hours 45 minutes

10. (a) (i) • Strategy: four points plotted correctly
    - Strategy: remaining three points plotted correctly
    (ii) • Acceptable line of best fit drawn
    (b) • Strategy: extend line of best fit and read graph
    - No, as the height will only be 2·36 metres at 0830

11. • 200 × 2·75 = 550
    - £13·75
    - 550 − 13·75 = 536·25
    - 700 − 536·25 = £163·75

12. • $\frac{15}{200}$
    - Strategy: know how to compare gradients
    - $\frac{15}{200} = 0·075$
    - Yes, 0·06 < 0·075 < 0·08

13. (a) • Strategy: know to add semi-circle and 3 straight edges
    - $\frac{1}{2} \times 3·14 \times 20 + 20 + 8 + 8 = 67·4$
    - 67·4 × 5 × 3 = (£)1011
    (b) • Strategy: any 7 boxes correct
    - Strategy: remaining 4 boxes correct
    (c) • Strategy: select critical path 2 + 4 + 2 + 1 + 2 + 1
    - No, because it will take 12 hours

Paper 2

1. • Strategy: identify multiplier 0·959
   - Strategy: identify power ...³
   - Calculate value 687939·7816
   - (£)688 000

2. • $\frac{24}{64}$ or equivalent
   - Mark on gauge consistent with working

3. (a) (i) • $(\bar{x} =)48·7$
   (ii) • Process: calculate $(x-\bar{x})^2$ 0·81, 0·16, 2·25, 0·64, 3·24, 0·64
   - Strategy: substitute into formula $\sqrt{\frac{7·74}{5}}$
   - Calculate standard deviation (s =) 1·24
   (b) Two valid comments:
   - Comment regarding the mean: on average, the athlete's times have increased after training with the coach.

138 ANSWERS FOR NATIONAL 5 APPLICATIONS OF MATHEMATICS

- Comment regarding standard deviation: the athlete's times are more consistent after training with the coach.

4.
- Strategy/process: interpret graph and state fraction for each type of car $\frac{30}{150}, \frac{65}{150}, \frac{55}{150}$ or equivalent
- Calculate angles 72°, 156°, 132°
- Construct pie chart and complete with labels

5. (a)
- Strategy: consider three options
- 210 or 210 or 252
- 252 (boxes)

   (b)
- £1755 + 252 × £2·99 = £2508·48
- £2508·48 ÷ 252 ÷ 4 = £2·49

6. (a)
- 0·12 × (42380 − 8060) = 4118·40
- 0·02 × (49920 − 42380) = 150·80
- 4118·40 + 150·80 = 4269·20

   (b)
- 0·09 × 49920 = 4492·80
- 49920 − (4492·80 + 4269·20 + 6870·04) = 34287·96
- (34287·96 ÷ 12) = 2857·33

   (c)
- 2857·33 − (750 + 450 + 625 + 125 + 350) = 557·33
- Yes, he will have enough.

7. (a)
- 22 ÷ 5 = 4·4 cm
  37 ÷ 5 = 7·4 cm
- Bearing of 045° (±1°) measured correctly and 4·4 cm (±0·1 cm) correctly drawn
- Bearing of 170° (±1°) measured correctly and 7·4 cm (±0·1 cm) correctly drawn

   (b)
- 314 (°)
- 6·1 cm so 30·5 miles

   (c)
- 30·5 + 22 + 37 = 89·5
- 8 hour 30 min − 4 hour 5 min = 4 hour 25 min
  $4\frac{25}{60} = 4\cdot416...$
- $\frac{89\cdot5}{4\cdot416...} = 20\cdot264...$ 20·26 mph

8. (a) (i)
- Strategy: identify the costs not included $32 and $37
- $114 + 32 + 37 = $183

   (ii)
- Strategy: identify the "missing" attraction and the two cheapest attractions $24, $32 and $30
- Calculate the cost for card 2: $71 + $24 + $32 + $30 = $157
- State cost of card 3: $180
- $157

   (b)
- Strategy: evidence of knowing to divide: 157 ÷ 100·96 or 100·96 ÷ 157
- £1 gives $1·555 or $1 gives £0·643

9. (a)
- Strategy/process: use Pythagoras Theorem to calculate hypotenuse 25
- 25 − 16 = 9(m)

   (b)
- Strategy: triangle − semi circle
- $\frac{1}{2} \times \pi \times 4\cdot5^2 = 31\cdot808...$
- 150 − 31·808... = 118·191...118·2(m²)

   (c)
- 118·2 ÷ 20 × 1000 = 5910
- 5910 ÷ 25 = 236·4, 237 bags
- 237 × 2·59 = (£)613·83

10. (a)
- Strategy: know how to use ratio
- 12000 + 4000 + 8000 = 24000 cm³
- 24000 ÷ 729 = 32·92… = 32 (candles)

   OR
- Strategy: know how to use ratio
- 12000 cm³ and 364·5
- 12000 ÷ 364·5 = 32·92 rounded to 32 (candles)

   (b)
- 3 × 13·75 + 32 × 0·18 = 47·01
- 47·01 × 1·65 = 77·57
- 77·57 ÷ 32 = 2·424… = (£)2·43/2·42

   (c)
- Strategy: knows how to find compound volume
- Strategy: substitute into cylinder formula V = π × 3·5 × 3·5 × 12
- 461·8 (or 461·58)
- Strategy: substitute into cone formula $V = \frac{1}{3}\pi \times 3\cdot5 \times 3\cdot5 \times 4$
- 51·3
- 461·8 + 51·3 = 513·1, 12000 ÷ 513·1 = 23·38
- No, he can't make 25 candles

NATIONAL 5 APPLICATIONS OF MATHEMATICS 2018

One mark is available for each •. There are no half marks.

Paper 1

1.
- Process: calculate 3% of 400 = 12
- Process: calculate max and min = 412 and 388
- Process: $\frac{4}{13}$ cakes will be rejected

2.
- Process: calculate cost of city break 270 + 90 × 4 + 450 + 30 = 1110
- Strategy/process: know how to find number of weeks
- Process/communication: Number of weeks = 23

3. (a)
- Communication: 4 points correct
- Communication: all 8 points correct

   (b)
- Communication: consistent line of best fit

   (c)
- Communication: answer consistent with line of best fit

4.
- Process: calculate new temperature = −28
- Communication: mark temperature on Celsius scale

5.
- Strategy: know how to add fractions
- Process: $\frac{3}{7} + \frac{1}{3} = \frac{9}{21} + \frac{7}{21} = \frac{16}{21}$
- Process: $\frac{5}{21}$

ANSWERS FOR NATIONAL 5 APPLICATIONS OF MATHEMATICS

OR
- Strategy: know how to convert a fraction to a decimal
- Process: 0·333... + 0·428... = 0·761...
- Process: 0·239 or 0·238

6.
- Strategy: 105 know correct order of operations
- Process/communication: 18·1 and consistent conclusion

7. (a) • Process: 750 × 9 = 6750
   (b) • Strategy/process: (6750 − 2700) ÷ 9 = 450
   • Process: 450 × 20 = 9000

8. • Strategy: know to calculate the sale price in two stages
   • Process: calculate 75% of the price = 525
   • Process: 498·75

9. • Strategy/process: 11:10 pm or equivalent
   • Strategy: e.g. 11:10 + 8 = 7:10 am
   or
   8:50 − 8 = 00:50 am
   or equivalent
   • Process: 1 hour 40 minutes

10. (a) • Process: find 80% of 35 = 28
    (b) • Strategy/process: calculate overall percentage = 67

11. • Strategy: know how to find perimeter
    3·14 × 20 + 34 + 34
    • Process: calculate semi circles 3·14 × 20 = 62·8
    • Strategy/process: 62·8 + 34 + 34 + 2·8 = 133·6

12. (a) • Process: 82 ÷ 10 rep by 8·2 cm
        46 ÷ 10 rep by 4·6 cm
    • Process/communication: Bearing of 042° (±1°) measured correctly and 8·2 cm (±0·1 cm) correctly drawn
    • Process/communication: Bearing of 194° (±1°) measured correctly and 4·6 cm (±0·1 cm) correctly drawn
    (b) • Process: bearing consistent with diagram
    • Process: distance consistent with diagram

13. • Strategy: $h^2 = 10^2 - 6^2$
    • Process: calculate height = 8
    • Process: calculate area 8 × 12 ÷ 2 = 48

14. • Strategy/process: know to find total number of combinations
    • Process: find the number of combinations less than 5 = 13
    • Communication: $\frac{13}{35}$

15. • Process: 25 cm = 0·25 m or 4 m = 400 cm
    • Communication: state gradient = $\frac{25}{400}$
    • Process/communication: Simplify $\frac{25}{400}$ to $\frac{1}{16}$
    Yes, $\frac{1}{16} < \frac{1}{14}$

Paper 2

1. (a) • Strategy: identify multiplier = 0·87
   • Strategy: identify power = ...³
   • Process: calculate value = 921·90(42)
   • Communication: round to 2 significant figures = 920
   (b) • Strategy: $\frac{450}{1400} \times 100$
   • Process: calculate percentage = 32(·1...)
   OR
   • Strategy: use trial and improvement
   • Process: calculate percentage = 32

2. (a) • Communication: Q_2 = 19
   • Communication: Q_1 = 11 and Q_3 = 24
   (b) • Communication: correct end points at 5 and 34
   • Communication: correct box showing Q_1, Q_2, Q_3

3. • Strategy: select correct two packages only = B and D
   • Process: calculate total cost of one package
   e.g. package B
   (8·95 + 20·99) × 12 + 59·99 = 419·27
   • Process/communication: calculate total cost of remaining package(s) and state cheapest package
   e.g. package D
   (7·99 + 18·99) × 12 + 109·99 = 433·75 **and** package B

4. (a) • Strategy: $\frac{144}{360} \times 105$
   • Process: calculate time in minutes = 42
   OR
   • 105 ÷ (360 ÷ 144)
   • Process: calculate time in minutes = 42
   (b) • Process: $\frac{21}{60}(= 0.35)$
   • Process: calculate distance
   6·6 × 0·35 = 2·31

5. (a) • Strategy: know to use inverse proportion
   • Process: 350 × 18 = 6300
   • Strategy/process: 6300 ÷ 450 = 14
   (b) • Strategy/process: V = π × 1·9² × 9·7
   • Process: calculate volume 110·009...m³

6. • Strategy/process: 154 ÷ 7 = 22
   • Strategy/process: total amount paid = 330

7. • Strategy/process: convert km to miles
   650 ÷ 1·609 = 403·977...
   • Strategy/process: convert litres to gallons
   50 ÷ 4·545 = 11
   • Strategy/process: calculate total distance possible on a full tank in miles
   47 × 11 = 517
   • Communication: Yes (since 404 < 517)
   OR
   • Strategy/process: convert litres to gallons
   50 ÷ 4·545 = 11
   • Strategy/process: calculate total distance possible on a full tank in miles
   47 × 11 = 517

140 ANSWERS FOR NATIONAL 5 APPLICATIONS OF MATHEMATICS

- Strategy/process: convert miles to km
  $517 \times 1\cdot609 = 831\cdot853$
- Communication: Yes (since 650 < 832)

OR

- Strategy/process: convert km to miles
  $650 \div 1\cdot609 = 403\cdot977...$
- Strategy/process: calculate number of gallons required
  $403\cdot977... \div 47 = 8\cdot595...$
- Strategy/process: convert gallons to litres
  $8\cdot595... \times 4\cdot545 = 39\cdot065...$
- Communication: Yes (since 39 < 50)

OR

- Strategy/process: convert km to miles
  $650 \div 1\cdot609 = 403\cdot977...$
- Strategy/process: calculate number of gallons required $403\cdot977... \div 47 = 8\cdot595...$
- Strategy/process: convert litres to gallons
  $50 \div 4\cdot545 = 11$
- Communication: Yes (since $8\cdot595 < 11$)

OR

- Strategy/process: convert miles per gallon to km per gallon $47 \times 1\cdot609 = 75\cdot623...$
- Strategy/process: convert litres to gallons
  $50 \div 4\cdot545 = 11$
- Strategy/process: calculate total distance possible on a full tank in km $11 \times 75\cdot623 = 831\cdot853$
- Communication: Yes (since $650 < 831\cdot853$)

8. (a) • Strategy: pick cheapest prices and add cost of frame
   - Process: find total cost = $2960\cdot39$
   (b) • Strategy: calculate finance package
   - Process: calculate deposit
   - Process: find total finance package
     $448\cdot65 + 36 \times 76\cdot50 = 3202\cdot65$
   - Communication:
     $3202\cdot65 - 2960\cdot39 = 242\cdot26$
   (c) (i) • Process: $(61\cdot2 + 58\cdot3 + 59\cdot1 + 58\cdot8 + 60\cdot4 + 59\cdot8) \div 6 = 59\cdot6$
       (ii) • Process: calculate
         $(x - \bar{x})^2$
         $= 2\cdot56, 1\cdot69, 0\cdot25, 0\cdot64, 0\cdot64, 0\cdot04$
   - Strategy/process: substitute into formula
     $\sqrt{(5\cdot82 \div 5)}$
   - Process: standard deviation = $1\cdot078...$

OR

- Process: calculate
  Σx and $\Sigma x^2 = 357\cdot6$ and $21318\cdot78$

- Strategy/process: substitute into formula
  $$\sqrt{\dfrac{2131878 - \dfrac{357\cdot6^2}{6}}{5}}$$
- Process: standard deviation = $1\cdot078...$

(d) • Communication: comment regarding mean e.g. on average, Scott's top speed is higher on his new bike
- Communication: comment regarding standard deviation e.g. top speed is more consistent with new bike

9. (a) • Strategy: correct letter **and** number in all boxes
   (b) • Strategy: select critical path $900 + 2 + 3 + 300 + 5 + 5$
   - Process/communication: yes, it takes 20 minutes 15 seconds

   OR

   yes, it takes 20·25 minutes

   (c) • Strategy: calculate the correct two ways of packing
   - Process: calculate number of boxes for one arrangement
     $240 \div 60 = 4$
     $1250 \div 40 = 31\cdot25$
     $260 \div 15 = 17\cdot3...$
     $17 \times 31 \times 4 = 2108$
   - Process/Communication: calculate second arrangement and state conclusion
     $240 \div 40 = 6$
     $1250 \div 60 = 20\cdot83...$
     $260 \div 15 = 17\cdot3...$
     $17 \times 6 \times 20 = 2040$
     Maximum – 2108 boxes

   (d) • Process: calculate the number of days and hours
     $277 \div 24 = 11$ days and 13 hours
   - Process: deal with journey time
     15th June at 1100
   - Process/Communication: date and time of arrival (taking into account time difference) = 15th June at 0600

   OR

   - Process: calculate the number of days and hours
     $277 \div 24 = 11$ days and 13 hours
   - Process: deal with time difference e.g.
     $2200 - 5$ hours = 1700
   - Process/Communication: date and time of arrival (taking into account journey time) = 15th June at 0600

10. (a) (i) • Strategy/process: $42\,000 - 8164 = 33\,836$
    - Process: calculate national insurance
      12% of $33\,836 = 4060\cdot32$

(ii) • Process: calculate annual net pay
42 000 − 5427·96 − 4060·32 − 3360 = 29151·72
 • Process: calculate monthly net pay
29151·72 ÷ 12 = 2429·31

(b) • Process: 2429·31 − 1714 = 715·31

(c) • Process: monthly cost of 1 bed apartment = 804·72
 • Process: monthly cost of the 3 bed farmhouse = 618·91
 • Communication: 3 bed farmhouse is cheapest

OR

 • Process: annual cost of 1 bed apartment or 3 bed farmhouse = 9656·64 or 7426·92
 • Process: annual cost of the remaining two = 7426·92 or 9656·64 and 8760
 • Communication: 3 bed farmhouse is cheapest

11. (a) • Process: calculate area of 2 longer walkways
$2 \times 17·5 \times 1·5 = 52·5$

or

$2 \times 16 \times 1·5 = 48$

 • Process: calculate total area
$52·5 + 8 \times 1·5 = 64·5$

or

$48 + 11 \times 1·5 = 64·5$

OR

 • Process: calculate area of shorter walkway
$11 \times 1·5 = 16·5$

or

$8 \times 1·5 = 12$

 • Process: calculate total area
$16·5 + 2 \times 16 \times 1·5 = 64·5$

or

$12 + 2 \times 17·5 \times 1·5 = 64·5$

OR

 • Process: calculate total area
$17·5 \times 11 = 192·5$
 • Process: calculate area of walkway
$192·5 − 8 \times 16 = 64·5$

(b) • Strategy: calculate number of boxes required
$64·5 \times 16 \div 50 (= 20·64)$
 • Process: appropriate rounding and calculate cost
$21 \times 71·95 = 1510·95$

(c) • Strategy: know how to find the volume
 • Process: calculate the volume of one part e.g.
$8 \times 0·5 \times 16 = 64$
 • Process: calculate volume of remaining part(s) and add

e.g. $\frac{1}{2} \times 12 \times 1·5 \times 8 + 64 = 136$

 • Process: convert to litres
$136 \times 100 \times 100 \times 100/1000 = 136\,000$

OR

 • Strategy: know how to find the volume
 • Process: calculate area of cross section

$\frac{1}{2} \times 12 \times 1·5 + 16 \times 0·5 = 17$

 • Process: calculate volume
$17 \times 8 = 136$
 • Process: convert to litres
$136 \times 100 \times 100 \times 100/1000 = 136\,000$

Acknowledgements

Permission has been sought from all relevant copyright holders and Hodder Gibson is grateful for the use of the following:

Image © Aleksander Krsmanovic/Shutterstock.com (2017 Paper 2 page 5);
Image © topae/Shutterstock.com (2017 Paper 2 page 10);
Image © Jodie Johnson/stock.adobe.com (2017 Paper 2 page 14);
Image © Baloncici/Shutterstock.com (2017 Paper 2 page 15);
Image © ibreakstock/Shutterstock.com (2017 SQP Paper 1 page 3);
Image © eugenesergeev/stock.adobe.com (2017 SQP Paper 2 page 7);
Image © eugenesergeev/stock.adobe.com (2018 Paper 2 page 14);
Image © Ewelina Wachala/Shutterstock.com (2018 Paper 2 page 18);
Image © Eunika Sopotnicka/123RF.com (2018 Paper 2 page 18);
Image © 1000 Words/Shutterstock.com (2018 Paper 2 page 18).